BILL T'S TEXAS BOB TALES

By
Bill R. Thomas

**With Illustrations By
Don Kirkland**

To My Dad and Granddad Thomas
(Great Story Tellers)

And a special thanks to my buddy,
Don Kirkland, for the illustrations.

THE MAIN INTRODUCTION

I grew up back in the sticks before television was available. In those days, folks entertained themselves by conversation. Generally, when a group gathered under the shade of a large oak tree in the summer or around the large pot bellied stove in Orange's store in the winter - someone would tell a "tall tale" to get the conversation going and before long everyone was trying to top the previous story with one of their own. My granddad, Lilbourne Thomas generally topped them all - followed closely by my dad, Otho Thomas.

With the advent of air conditioning, good highways, fast cars, and television - story telling has become a lost art in our society. It's sad that the younger generation didn't experience the fun of this form of live entertainment.

Some of the stories I heard in my youth served as an inspiration for this book. I have rewritten some of the stories as I remember them (i.e. Old Wolf, The Automatic Pump Shotgun, etc.) plus added a few of my own which are based on actual experiences I have enjoyed while pursuing my first love - hunting and fishing in the great out of doors.

All my life I have been an avid reader. Even today, I prefer to plop down in my favorite recliner and read a good book over watching most of the crap broadcast on T.V. (The two exceptions being a Cowboy football game and an old John Wayne movie).

Several years ago I was a member and director of a sports club called Dallas Woods and Waters. The Club's monthly magazine "The Banner" consisted of hunting and fishing stories submitted by its members. I was so critical of the magazine that they strongly suggested I write some stories if I was so darn good. Well, I did and most everyone thought they were pretty good. One day, someone else said, you should publish your stories in a book. So, I did.

Almost forgot to explain the title. These are short stories or <u>Bobbed</u> Tales in Texas, we refer to a dog or a cat that has had its tail cut off as being bobbed tailed or simply "Bobtail" - get it.

Also, I've assumed that sooner or later a tenderfoot may lay hands on this old book and start reading it - and trying to understand it! For his (or her) benefit. I've written a brief introduction before each category of stories.

Although I was born in the commonwealth of Kentucky I have spent all of my adult life in the great State of Texas. My wife is a native Texan (as are my children and grandchildren) but I am a Texan - by choice.

In the early days of my CPA career I traveled extensively across Texas - always carrying my fishing and hunting gear with me and using them at every opportunity, some of these stories came from these travels.

Substantially all of the body of these stories are based upon my experiences (with certain embellishments of course). I have changed the names of the people (most are dead) to protect their offspring. Some of the locations have been moved a tad also.

Most of these characters in the stories have been given a copy of the manuscript and they tell me things like "I didn't say that", or "That story didn't end like you wrote it", that didn't happen in that location, etc., etc. I respond "Heck, I know that - but this makes better reading. I freely admit that many of the punch lines and colorful expressions were pulled from my memory - I have no idea as to their origin. I put them in this book for you to enjoy - so enjoy.

Bill R. Thomas

TABLE OF CONTENTS

TABLE OF CONTENTS - Continued

A. DEER CAMP TALES

Texas and Texans solved the landowner/hunter problem many years ago with the "hunting lease." Under this arrangement, the landowner gives a group of hunters the right to hunt on his property for one hunting season for a fixed amount of dollars. There are all sorts of modifications but what I just said are the terms of a basic hunting lease. Usually the landlord will limit the number of hunters (guns) which may use the lease.

Since these leases are rather expensive, usually one hunter or a small group of hunters will put together a hunting group of several hunters to buy the lease.

Many (if not most) deer hunters will skip around from one lease to another from year to year - because they didn't see enough game on the prior lease, there was some hunter they didn't like on the lease, someone snored too loud on the lease, etc., etc.

Some of the leases had some sort of crude facility for the hunters (old barn, old "hired hand shack," etc.) but most had nothing. Some allowed you to "stalk" hunt but most required that you stay in a "deer stand." (In addition to the land owners rules - the hunting group usually came up with their own rules).

But the one universal thing about every deer lease I ever hunted on was the bull crap stories and pranks that went on around deer camp. The following stories were taken from my memories of deer hunts and deer camps past.

CHAPTER 1

A Friendly Poker Game at Deer Camp

The winter of 1945 was extra cold – and long – in West Kentucky. We lived on a scrubby hillside farm – poor but happy. The "Big War" was over and items which had been in short supply or not available during the war were beginning to appear at O'Brian's Hardware Store. The time seemed right for my friend Rodney Earl "Rod" Lamb, and me to get serious about our plans to spend the summer of 1946 on Piney Creek. We were both 14 and had not developed more than a curiosity about girls so a summer away from civilization seemed like a very good idea.

Rod's uncle had a saw mill and he agreed to saw out some suitable lumber for a boat if we provided the trimmed logs. There were a couple of large popular trees in a patch of woods by our horse lot and my dad agreed that we could cut them if we would burn the trimmings and clean out the woods some. Rod and I sawed the two popular trees down in early winter and trimmed them out and let them season that winter. The following spring my Uncle Calvin brought his old Ford flat-bed truck by on Sunday and we hauled them to the saw mill.

In about a month Rod said that the boards were ready for our boat building project so we decided to build the boat in his dad's barn since it was closest to the sawmill. We had spent several months designing and redesigning the craft and had finally settled on the "perfect boat" for us – a 16ft flat bottom with a semi-pointed front end.

The boards were rough cut sawmill variety and the first thing we had to do was spend hours shaving them down – by hand. We next started measuring and cutting them by hand – and putting our boat together. We commenced to nail it together but some expert looked at it and told us the nails would rust out and the boat would come apart in no time. We ended up buying some brass screws at the hardware store in Princeton and pulling out the nails and replacing them with the screws.

When we finally got it put together it was, even if I say so, a fine looking boat. We filled (and refilled, and refilled) it with water and let it "swell." We next filled the cracks with hemp and tar. Finally she was leak proof and sea worthy. We next sanded it real good and painted it barn red with some paint that one of Rod's uncles donated to us.

Finally, the day we had worked for all winter and spring arrived – launch day. Several of our friends were rounded up on Saturday morning to help us carry the boat from the barn to the Tradewater River which was about a quarter mile away. We had built some boat paddles out of the "extra" popular boards and the minute we got to the river both Rod and I jumped in and started paddling – she floated and was truly sea worthy and easy to maneuver. We spent most of that day giving our helpers boat rides.

The next couple of weekends we went on short fishing trips and got to know her better. One thing became obvious – it was going to be one long, many paddle stroke, trip to our permanent camp at the mouth of Piney Creek – about ten miles distant.

It's funny how Lady Luck can smile on you – just at the right time. A classmate, Cornall Taylor had an old Evinrude outboard motor (about 2 or 3 horsepower – exposed fly wheel and all) that his granddad had given him and I had a 12 gauge single barrel shotgun that Cornall wanted real bad. The trade was made and we bolted our new "paddles" to the transom of our new boat. The motor was somewhat cantankerous and hard to start but if you nursed the choke and didn't get in a big hurry – after it fired up, it purred like a kitten but smoked like a freight train. We were now set for our great adventure and could hardly wait for school to let out for the summer.

We had been getting all our other gear patched up and ready for the great expedition and adventure which lay ahead. Our parents had agreed that we could spend a few weeks in the summer on the creek provided the crops were in and we would come back to the farm occasionally and do our share of the cultivating.

The final week of school seemed like an eternity – minutes became hours and hours became days. Finally – school "let out" for the summer. We already had our gear stashed in the corn crib at the Lamb's farm and it didn't take me long to trot home, change, say goodbye to my folks, and literally run to the Lamb's place down the road. Rod had already packed one load of gear to the river when I arrived and was getting together his second load when I pulled up to a stop – huffing and puffing. After I got my wind I gathered up an armful of gear and we headed for the river – loaded down with tent, skillet, pots, pans, 22 rifles, etc.

There was less than another load of stuff remaining so I agreed to go back to the house and get it while he packed the boat and warmed up the Evinrude. I ran back to the house and picked up the balance of our provisions – mostly groceries – lard, bacon, eggs, flour, corn meal, molasses, jellies, etc. and hurried back to the "dock" – an old beech tree on the bank where we tied up the boat. This was about two miles upriver from Dawson Springs. Rod was anxiously awaiting my arrival – the boat was untied and being held to the bank by the running outboard – I "threw" the groceries in and jumped aboard and shoved us away from the bank. Before we were two feet from the bank, Rod's old half breed spotted dog, name of Chester, jumped in the boat on top of our supplies and very nearly capsized us. We drifted out, when Rod, who was in the back of the boat operating the Evinrude, immediately "opened her up."

In hindsight we couldn't have been moving more than 5 knots (loaded and going against the current). However, I assure you that we felt the exhilaration of speed and excitement as great as that felt by the modern day fisherman in the fastest bass boat on the water.

Soon the scent along the river bank started changing – from civilized fields of crops and pastures with cattle in them to "natural" woodlands. In the first half hour we had seen three squirrels and a rabbit along the river bank. We rounded a bend in the river and passed under the Messamore bridge and knew that about ¼ of our journey was behind us. Later the mouth of Montgomery Creek loomed ahead – where it emptied into the river, and we knew we were half way there as we drew past Montgomery Creek, a deer had appeared on the bank and Chester saw it. He howled and jumped in the river and swam toward the deer. I yelled "Chester – come back here". Rod said "Let him go – he'll chase that deer a while then go back to the house – and good riddance". The excitement continued to mount.

There were no more farms between us and Piney Creek so the river banks were completely wooded the balance of our journey. We soon lost count of squirrels and had seen deer, mink, beaver, muskrat, and coons. We were in the Pennyrile Forest which was Federal government land – bought up during the depression years and preserved as a hardwood forest. We didn't talk much (shout I mean) during the trip. Despite the small size, the Evinrude made a helluva racket and you had to shout to be heard above its pop! popping noise.

As we got closer to Piney, we decided to try to get a squirrel for super so we shut the Evinrude down and paddled for a while – it didn't take long to slip up on a squirrel which was up a tree leaning out over the river and in one shot from the trusty Winchester single shot 22, Rod had the meat for our supper. Rod fired up the Evinrude again and soon the large rock jutting up in the river (called the "Devils Dining Table") announced that Piney was just around the next bend. By now the sun was starting to set and we knew we would have to work fast to get our camp in order and our beds fixed before it got dark.

The banks of the river and Piney Creek were tall rock bluffs – up to 100 ft. tall at the place where Piney entered the river. These same type of banks were along Piney Creek for about the first mile and a half before the ground kind of leveled out along the creek bank for the next three or four miles and then kind of turned into swamp land. There weren't any roads into the area so the only way in was to walk or come by boat as we had. We didn't expect many visitors.

Rod guided the boat into Piney Creek and it seemed like we were down in a deep hole – the creek was only about a third as wide as the river and the bluffs were even taller on both sides of the creek. We went up the creek about half a mile and Rod eased the boat over to the east bank where a rock ledge stood out about a foot above the water level. I took the rope attached to the front of our boat in my hand and jumped out on the ledge and secured the rope to the large rock. Rod started handing the gear from the boat while I stacked it on the ledge – a "natural" boat dock. As the last parcel was unloaded. Rod climbed out, stretched his legs and let out a "rebel yell" – we were finally "home" for the summer. (We had camped out at this spot before and I still consider it the best campsite I have ever used – however, today the entire area is now covered by the waters of Lake Beshear and I'll never see it again.- except in my mind.)

About ten fee above the "boat dock" ledge was another ledge and at the back of it was a shallow cave named "Bandit Cave" – said to be hideout of the Jessie James gang at one time. There are probably dozens of such caves in Kentucky, Tennessee. Arkansas, Missouri and Kansas (where the James gang traveled) – and many are named Bandit's Cave. That was to be our summer "house." Years ago some one had hacked out steps in the sandstone and there was a crude rail rigged up to hold on to as you climbed up to the second ledge. The only problem with our campsite was – no firewood. We had picked up a couple of dead tree limbs back down the river where I shot the squirrel but knew they would not last long – enough fire to cook supper and that was about it.

We started transferring our gear to the upper ledge (I pulled most of it up by rope – I stood on the upper ledge and Rod stayed below and would tie it to the rope when I threw it down.) By the time we were finished it was dark and we were operating by the light of the old battered kerosene lantern we had brought. We didn't own a flashlight but had a carbide lamp in addition to the lantern.

Rod build a makeshift fireplace and started the fire while I started "organizing" our camp – placing the "army surplus" bags in the cave – stacking the other gear so I could find it. While I was doing this Rod was down by the boat – cleaning the squirrel and setting out a couple of bank lines. He used the squirrel "entrails" for bait. By the time he was finished I already had a skillet of potatoes and onions on the fire and the skillet of grease ready for the squirrel. Since it was getting late I decided to salt and pepper the meat and cook it without flour. Before long we were sitting by the fire with out legs crossed Indian style – dining on fried squirrel and my now famous hash browned potatoes and onions. The stars were out bright and it was a perfect night. We sat and talked until our supply of firewood was gone and the fire had burned down to coals.

We did not realize that it was getting quite late and we were tired – the adrenalin had been flowing long and strong. However, within minutes of slipping into our sleeping bags and blowing out the lantern – we were both fast asleep. As usual, at first light I was wide awake and got up first. I was a little stiff from sleeping on solid rock. I was eager to get busy with the days chores – making our camp more comfortable and livable. I got dressed and climbed down the steps to the boat dock, intending to use the boat to go scouting for some firewood. It was light enough to see the outline of the bluffs and tree lines but still too dark to see any "details" down in the canyon so I had to feel my way around. I got into the boat and while "feeling" for the rope to untie it I felt one of the bank lines which Rod had set out – it was alive! Whoopee! I let out a holler and woke Rod up. He came scrambling down the steps in his shorts as I was pulling the line in. When I got the fish out of the water I could tell it was a nice one that was fighting to stay in the creek. Since it was still too dark to do anything with the fish we decided to leave him in the water hooked to the throw line. Rod checked the other line and said it also had a fish on it but didn't pull him in. We both got in the boat and cast off to go get firewood. Rod was in the back of the boat trying to get the Evinrude started and I was in the front of the boat – paddling to get us out into the current. The current soon carried us to the mouth of the creek and I paddled across the river to a wooded bank and hopped out and tied us up. Rod was still twisting the Evinrude's tail but without success.

Since Rod was barefoot and in his shorts and was cold and shaking in the back of the boat – pulling on the start rope every now and then between cuss words – it fell my task to stumble through the woods and gather some firewood. I made three or four trips and had a good boatload by the time Rod had the old outboard engine running. It was good daylight when I climbed into the front of the boat and we headed back to camp. When we pulled up to the dock the boat evidently scared the fish cause the line were really cutting up. We threw the firewood on to the ledge and climbed out and each got a fish line and started to pull the fish in. I got my fish in first – about a ten pound catfish. Rod's turned out to be around six or seven pounds – also a catfish.

It was my turn to clean fish so Rod got dressed, built a fire, and cooked breakfast while I cleaned the two catfish. By the time I was finished, the fried bacon and eggs and coffee were ready. As we ate we started planning all the camp projects that lay ahead:

- Build two beds
- Connect the tent across the cave entrance
- Build a permanent fireplace and oven
- Build a table and chairs
- Build shelves to keep our stuff out of reach of field mice, etc.

As the days passed necessity dictated that we add other projects to our list. By the end of our stay – we had all the comforts of home.

After the planning session we unpacked our gear and sorted it out into three basic piles –

(a) Camping gear
(b) Cooking gear and supplies, and
(c) Hunting and fishing gear

The camping gear included some army surplus stuff – pup tent, sleeping bag, pick/shovel, canteens, and water cans along with an old battered kerosene lantern, two carbide lamps and carbide canisters, 4 candles, box of matches, rope, nails, wire, etc., a single bit ax, and a hatchet.

The cooking gear included a large cast iron skillet, and a cast iron dutch oven, a baking pan, old coffee pot, 2 army mess kits, several coffee cans, mason jars, knives, forks, spoons, and a couple of dish rags. The hunting and fishing gear consisted of two single shot .22 caliber rifles, 4 boxes of .22 shells, a roll of stagin (fishing line), a jar of lead sinkers which we had made by melting the lead from an old car battery and a jar of assorted fish hooks.

The next order of business was to get our week's supply of water. There was a good spring about a half mile down the Tradewater past the Piney Creek cut off. We got the army surplus water cans, hopped in the boat, and made the water haul.

When we got back we started on our "projects" – beginning with the cave (our summer "home").

CHAPTER 2

PUT UP OR SHUT UP

I was not long out of the Air Force and new to Dallas (1957). The city was really growing and expanding in those days and I began to have an urge to go hunting that fall. I was a staff accountant (audit) for a large C.P.A. firm and one day at coffee break at a clients office one of the client employees was talking about hunting and fishing. I joined the group and sort of worked my way into the discussion.

When I asked "Where can you hunt around Dallas if you don't own a farm or have a hunting lease? (I had already learned about Texas "hunting leases" - a totally new concept to me). A fellow standing next to me said "Dallas Wood and Waters - DWWC." I asked "What is that?" And he explained that it was a hunting and fishing club in Dallas that took hunting and fishing trips. I said "That sounds too expensive for me." He said "No it isn't - I'm a member." He invited me to attend their next meeting as his guest - which I promptly accepted.

The DWWC met monthly at noon at a local hotel. I met my "sponsor" at the next meeting. We sat at the table with some of the "old timers" - one (Roger Godwin) of which took me under wing. His home was close to mine in East Dallas. The program was good and the food was delicious and the DWWC had a new member - me. When I learned of how the DWWC operated and they had an upcoming hunting trip (Dove hunt) in just a couple of weeks - I promptly signed up for that too. Their mode of operations was very simple - a "trip chairman" organized each trip and made all the arrangements. After a sign up period, the total cost of the trip was divided by the number making the trip - and that was the cost. (very reasonable.)

Most of the old heads, including Roger, at our table were signed up for the dove hunt. Since you had to provide your own transportation to Throckmorton (location of the dove hunt), Roger invited me to ride with him and a couple of his friends. I accepted - providing they let me drive my vehicle - a nearly new 4 wheel drive INTERNATIONAL SCOUT. They leaped at the offer.

I asked what I should bring and they said - your gun, some snake proof boots, canteen and ice chest. We would be staying at a motel and eating out except for the big feed that the rancher, Hartsell Ash, would provide the last night. I told them my guns were back in Kentucky with my parents one of them asked "Can't you borrow a shotgun from someone?" (I forgot to mention - during the meal I had bragged on what a great shot I was - even won the Kentucky marksmanship contest - blah, blah, blah.) I thought about who I might borrow a shotgun from and it hit me and I said "My neighbor who lives on the other side of the duplex showed me his shotgun the other day - it is a .410 single shot. The feller said "That would be perfect for a champion marksman like you." (I thought I heard a snicker but was not sure).

On the appointed day and time I loaded my .410 shotgun, a box of shells (25), canteen, hunting clothes and boots, and a small ice chest into the SCOUT and drover to Roger's house to pick him up. He was ready and eager to go but it looked like he was going on a 2 week vacation - judging by the stuff he loaded. he had a beautiful leather gun case, two canvas suitcases, and a full size ice chest. He gave me directions to the other two dove hunters and when we picked them up - same baggage. This presented a problem. The SCOUT had ample room for 4 people but very limited storage space. The fourth hunter had some rope so we tied most of their luggage on the roof rack - then headed west.

About every 30 miles I had to pull over and stop and one of them would get out and get four ice cold Lone Star beers out of an ice chest. Sometimes all four got out and we bled our lizards." It was during one of those stops that Roger look down at his lizard and said "George (that's what he called his lizard). I had a birthday last Sunday and if you hadn't died fifteen years ago you would have been 75 years old." We all got a big laugh - matter of fact - there were many funny jokes told on that trip and we had been laughing a lot. Soon we rolled into Throckmorton, Texas - the home of Bob Lilly (Dallas County).

We were the first to arrive at the Cowboy Motel so we had our pick on rooms. We picked 4 in a row on the west side and unloaded. It was probably around 4 p.m. - and hunting season did not start until noon the next day. After we settled in there was a knock or my door and my compadres wanted to go "check in" with the rancher on whose property we would be hunting and then go eat supper.

The ranch was right outside of town and the rancher, Hartsell Ash, was puttering around a large fireplace outside when we drove up. He appeared genuinely pleased to see us and when we were introduced I gave him my strongest grip and he countered. I liked him instantly and I believe the feeling was mutual. While we were visiting, his wife Margie, came out from the house and I was introduced to her. She gave me a big hug. (west Texas hospitality).

We invited them to join us for supper and they accepted. Roger suggested we eat at a cafe he liked in Haskell (about 30 miles west). The SCOUT would only hold us 4 so Hartsell and Margie followed in his pick up. Roger's choice was a good one - especially their homemade pies.

When we got back to the motel we each went to our room to watch T.V., read, or whatever. The next morning (early) there were knocks on my door and we loaded up and went to the Dairy Queen for breakfast. It was packed with locals. When we got back to the motel there were several cars in the parking spots - mostly Cadillac's and Lincolns. My bunch wanted to load their hunting stuff into the SCOUT and did. One of them said he was going to watch the locals play dominos and I joined him. Roger and the other man said they would hang around the motel or bum a ride to Hartsell's. We agreed to meet at Hartsell's at 11 a.m.

We went to the Domino Parlor and watched the locals play 42. They were playing for a penny a point. There were 4 games going on. One player left and the call went out for a player to step up and I did (I had played 42 all my life) when I quit at 10:45 they owed me $1.17. We went by the motel - no one there so we went on to the Ash Ranch. We joined the 48 other hunters and listened to Hartsell's instructions.

He got in his pick up and lead us to the hunting fields - about 5 miles down a gravel road. On the way, one of the men asked "Bill, how many shells do you think it will take you to kill 10 doves?" I replied "10 unless I get lucky and get 2 with 1 shot." They laughed but the one who asked said "Tell you what I'll do - if you get 10 with 10 shots, I'll clean your birds and buy you a case of Lone Star Beer." I asked "If I don't?" He said - you clean my birds and buy the beer." I said "You are on." The other two said they wanted a "piece of the action." I said "Fine with me."

When we got to the hunting fields Hartsell had opened a gate and everyone was parking in a cleared "parking lot" he had scraped out for that purpose. I started to park but Roger said "No - No". He pointed toward a utility tower about a mile west and said "Drive toward that tower - but put it in 4 wheel drive first." I did and in a few minutes we came upon a field of about 20 acres of freshly harvested milo. Dozens of Doves flushed out of the field. I parked under a mesquite.

There was a lone mesquite tree near the center of the field and mesquite trees grow along the fence lines. They told me my hunting spot was the tree in the center and they would be strung out along the fence. I said fine and climbed the fence with my .410, a box of shells, and canteen of water. They went marching off down the fence line packing automatic 12 gauge shotguns, folding stools that had a water proof pouch that held at least a six pack, and a canvass bag containing at least 4 boxes of shotgun shells.

I chuckled to myself as I headed toward center stage and they to front row seats. I was going to be the "show" (my dove shooting) and you can bet they would be watching every shot I made. There were a lot of high weeds growing under that lonesome mesquite tree and as soon as I took one step into the weeds to get into the shade and set up to shoot doves I heard the scary sound of a rattlesnake buzzing. Now I understood why the snake proof boots. My hair stood on end as I loaded a shotgun shell into the .410 and used the barrel to very carefully part the weeds as I searched for the snake. I finally located him close to the tree trunk - coiled and ready to strike. I cocked the hammer on the .410 and struck first. I knew the others would be wondering what I shot at for no doves had flown over so I picked the snake up by the tail and stepped out where they could see me and held it up - it was about 5 feet long. I cut off the rattle and dropped it in my pocket and threw the snake out into the field.

I got back under the tree and in a while I heard one of them yell "Doves" and I spotted them flying from north to south (where the others were located). There were about 10 doves in the bunch and they were out of my gun range so I didn't shoot - but the others did - about 9 shots - and 1 bird fell. I thought "lucky shot - they were out of their range too.

"Doves" they yelled again and I looked to the north and here came 3 more - they would pass to the west of me - in range. I cocked the .410 and waited till they were flying past - swing my gun and led the front bird and pulled the trigger - dead bird! I decided my best shots would be passing shots to the west where I would be swinging to my left - I wouldn't shoot any other shots.

To make the story short - the doves were plentiful and were flying back into the field to feed and by taking only relatively easy passing shots - eight shots later I had 9 doves. The old hunters had whooped and yelled at the first 5 or 6 shots but had quitted down - but shot many times. Matter of fact, there was a lot of shooting all around - it sounded like a war.

I was feeling purty good about myself and my next shot was a head on shot which I either missed or a miracle occurred - the dove kept right on flying. When I missed another they really hoorayed - and continued to do so after every shot from then on I missed the next 13 and was out of shells so I took my birds back to the SCOUT, cleaned them, got a beer, and turned on the radio and listened to a football game.

About 5:30 P.M. two of the hunters walked up and each had 10 birds. They drank beer, and hoorayed me as I cleaned their birds. When I finished I asked "Where is Roger?" They said he only had 4 birds when they left him and he would probably hunt till dark. I asked if they wanted me to take them back to the motel. They said no - the other hunters would get upset if we drove out and scared the birds. So we walked around, drank beer, and smoked for over an hour and Roger appeared. He was through for the day. I quickly cleaned his 6 birds, and we headed back to Throckmorton. A deer jumped in front of us and I swerved to miss him and almost wrecked - but didn't.

One of the hunters wanted to stop at a store and while he was getting some stuff I went in and bought a case of Lone Star Beer. I took the beer to the SCOUT and said "Fellows, I lost the bet and have cleaned your birds - and here is the beer I owe you." One of them gave me a funny look and said "Partner, you better listen better next time - you owe each of us a case of beer." So I went back and bought two more cases.

(Lesson learned - you cannot learn a thing with your mouth open and your jaws flapping - so shut up and listen).

When we got back to the motel the fellow that got the stuff at the store built a charcoal fire in a small grill he has brought and cooked a "mess" of doves for our supper. They were very good. I watched him as he fixed them. First, he wrapped a strip of bacon around each and fastened it with tooth picks. Next he put a very generous coating of creamy Italian salad dressing on each and placed them on the grill. He turned them frequently and kept pouring the creamy Italian on them. He opened a couple of cans of pork and beans and sat them on the grill to warm up. It was a very good meal but not in the same league as the next nights supper.

The next day was nearly a duplicate of the first day except I drove all over the countryside looking for .410, shells - no luck. Roger loaned me his spare shotgun and 2 boxes of shells. (12 gauge)   When we went to the hunting area and drove back to the milo field about 25 hunters had beat us to it. There was a Chevrolet suburban parked in the shade. Apparently most of the birds were concentrated in that area and word had gotten out.

Roger said "There's too many hunters here - let's try another spot" and he gave me directions. We ended at an old abandoned farm house that had about ten acres of Milo plus a small lake and many small "wooded" areas of mesquite trees. A few birds flew when we drove up. This time we split up - Roger went to the tank and the other two went out into the Milo Field. I picked a shady spot behind an old grain tank near the house - there was grain scattered on the bare ground near the tank. I shot about 10 times and got 7 birds - then Roger joined me - no action at the tank.

The "action" was much slower that second day but we got several birds and quit early - probably 4 p.m. We cleaned our birds and went back to the motel to wash up before going out to Hartsell's ranch.

When we drove up, Hartsell was out by his fireplace busily cooking. A few of the hunters were there visiting with him and we joined them. He showed us the steaks that he was going to cook later and asked if anyone would like some hors d' oeuvres. One hunter asked "What you got?" Heartsell winked at Roger and smilingly replied "Calf fries." (I knew immediately that this was part of the imitation of the first time city hunters). But I knew what "Calf Fries" were and I liked them so I spoke up and said "I would like about a half dozen." And a couple of the other hunters also ordered. Hartsell put a pot of grease on the fire and when it got hot he went to an ice chest and got a bowl of breaded Calf fries and dropped them into the hot grease.

In a minute or two Hartsell handed me a paper plate with 6 golden browned Calf fries and a thick slice of onion. I got a cold beer and found a shady spot to sit down and waited for them to cool down enough to eat and ate them all. They were delicious but I noticed all the old heads were poking one another, pointing at me and snickering. One of the men who had ordered some was out in the weeds throwing up. When I had cleaned my plate Hartsell asked "Want some more Bill?" I answered "Sure, and took my plate and he served six more." Roger asked "Boy, do you know what you are eating?" I said "Roger, I'm a country boy - these are what makes the difference between a bull and a steer." Hartsell laughed and said "He'll do." As he popped a Calf fry into his mouth and started to chew.

I went on many of the Dallas Woods and Waters trips over the years and recommend them very highly. They are still an active organization in Dallas.

CHAPTER 3

CUT THE DECK - LOW CARD COOKS

We bought into a deer lease down near San Saba one year and they had a peculiar rule about cooking. The first night on the lease, everybody gathered in the cook tent and cut a card out of the poker deck, whoever drew the lowest card had to do the camp cooking. However, the first person to complain automatically became cook and the other feller was relieved of his duties.

This particular lease was fairly big and there were about 15 hunters on it - mostly from Houston and San Antonio. We were the only three from Dallas.

According to the rules, we gathered around the first night and dutifully cut cards. Poor ole Slim cut a deuce and became the cook. He cussed and fussed but finally accepted his fate. The next morning he was up an hour before everyone else, fixing coffee and frying bacon and eggs. Everyone got up and ate and bragged on his cooking before they went off to hunt. Slim loved to hunt and was cussing cause he was going to be last to leave camp to hunt and he just knew some one of the bunch would go to the hunting area he had scouted out the day before and decided to hunt. And he was right - when he got there two of the Houston hunters were already hunting the area.

There were 8 - or 10 deer killed opening morning and we had plenty of back strap venison for several meals. Slim didn't care for venison and privately warmed himself a can of chili for supper that night and figured out a way to get out of his cooking chores. He took the back strap that he was going to cook and put it in a pot and soaked it in vinegar - then he poured a whole box of salt on it before he cooked it. He warmed up a large can of ranch beans and fixed a salad to go with the meat and beans.

Everyone came in and sat down to supper. They filed their plates with meat, beans, and salad. The first person to take a bite of the venison just happened to be one of the Houston hunters (who had invaded Slims hunting territory). When he put the chunk of meat into his mouth he yelled "Gracious - that's the saltiest durn meat I ever tasted" - all eyes turned to him and he suddenly repaired his mistake and quickly followed up with - "But that's just the way I like it."

Slim didn't lose his job and he got crankier and crankier. Most of the hunters saw how much it was bothering him so they started pulling pranks on him. They would hide stuff from the kitchen, leave him notes requesting certain menus, etc. - one such note requested Chocolate pie.

The next day Slim asked to borrow the keys to my pickup - explaining he had to go to town for a few "groceries." He was gone for about an hour and when he returned to camp he went straight to the cook tent with the groceries and closed the flap - in a while smoke started rising out of the stove pipe. Ken and I got curious and eased over to the cook shack but couldn't get in - the flap was tied on the inside. I said "Slim, let us in, it's Bill and Ken." He let us in and tied the flap behind us. I said "What in tarnation are you doing?" And he said "Making chocolate pies." Ken said "How moving" As he examined the pile of ex-lax wrappers on the table. Slim said "Unless you want a real moving experience - don't eat any chocolate pie." We had already decided we were not going to eat any. Slim burned the wrappers and said, those pies will come out of the oven in ten minutes and we can go hunting.

We got our guns and decided to hunt together that afternoon in an area on the ranch where Ken had seen a large buck on two or three occasions but had not been able to get a shot at him. The area had a long deep draw in it and our strategy was to have Slim circle around and find a stand up near the head of the draw. Ken and I would each go up one side of the draw and maybe drive a buck out so Slim could shoot it. After we had worked our way 3 or 4 hundred yards up the draw I heard something up ahead and saw a flash of white. I signaled Ken and we kept moving and in a minute heard K-Boom! - Splat! up ahead.

Sure enough, when we got there Slim was leaning over a real nice 10 point buck he had downed. He looked up at us and grinned like a possum eating chocolate pie and said "He's a dandy - thanks boys." We spent the next hour field dressing the buck and then dragging him to the road. I walked back to camp and got the pickup and came back and we loaded the deer.

Ken and I volunteered to haul Slims deer to the locker plant and Slim said he would go on back to camp and fix supper. Ken said "Don't fix anything for us - we'll eat in town." Slim said - "Good idea." We both knew we couldn't keep a straight face when the chocolate pie was served.

The next morning, there was a light turn out for breakfast. As soon as one of them took a few swigs of coffee they would grab a roll of toilet paper and head for the woods. A couple of them didn't quite make it and messed in their drawers. That day at noon we saw them huddled up and have a big pow wow.

At supper that night the results of the pow wow became obvious. The tall dog in the pack (leader), a big feller from Houston, stood up at the table and had a paper sack in his hand. He asked Slim to stand up and Slim did. We didn't know what to expect - a woodshed lecture or a much obliged. The ole boy from Houston kind of hemmed and hawed and beat around every bush in the county before he come to the point and said "Slim, we know you didn't want the cooks job and we've hoorayed you purty good - but you've been a real good sport about it. Here's a little gift the boys got for you and we promise we won't make sport with you again. He handed Slim the sack. Slim opened it and inside was a pair of the purtiest Nocona Boots you ever laid eyes on. Slim was really moved

- 28 -

as he looked around the tent at everyone and said "Thanks fellers - I appreciate this and I promise - if there's no more jokes - then no more pee in the soup."

We broke camp and headed home on that one.

CHAPTER 4

A TROPHY HUNT

Needless to say, they wouldn't let us renew on the San Sasa lease and Slim messed around the next year and didn't get us on a deer lease. He called me in late October and was in a panic. I finally got him settled down long enough to listen and asked him "would you and Ken be interested in trophy hunting this year." He said "Shoot yes, if it ain't as expensive as popcorn at a new picture show." I said, let me do some checking and I'll call you back.

I had an oil company client that had a big lease down near Del Rio that was under a game management program and produced some large Trophy bucks. The company used the lease primarily to entertain customers and my client had mentioned to me once that the lease was rarely used after the Thanksgiving weekend. I figured that for $750 each, they would let us hunt the lease all of December. I called my client and he agreed except we had to promise to "take care" of any of his customers if they showed up while we were there. Deal.

November 7th rolled around before you knew it and Slim called me and said "Today is opening day of deer season and do you realize this is the first time in fifteen years that me and you and Ken ain't opened deer season together – do you reckon that feller would let us go hunting next weekend?" I said "No Slim – a deal is a deal – be patient – we can go down December 1st but not until." He said "What are we going to do Thanksgiving weekend?" I told him my uncle had a small farm near Montalba and we could go over there and squirrel hunt to sharpen up our shooting eye if he wanted to ." He said "Let's do it – I'm going stir crazy around this house."

The three of us went squirrel hunting and driving back made plans for the big Trophy hunt. The next day I went by my clients and got a map of the ranch, lock combinations, etc. David my client, told me that we should just "Make ourselves at home when we got there – stay in the lodge, use whatever food, etc. was there etc. The name of the place was the Double Eagle Ranch and it was about 11 miles N.E. of Del Rio on FM 2523. The owner Rayl Ramirez lived in Del Rio. David's last words were don't shoot any of senor Ramirez' cows!

I picked up Ken and Slim in Fort Worth the next Friday afternoon and we headed south in my Ford pickup. We were traveling "light" since we were not going to need all our camping gear. Right after dark we all were hungry enough to eat the blade off a windmill so we stopped in Brady and ate a big steak supper. We filled up with gasoline and Ken took over as driver as we continued south. Ken was fast as small town gossip but it was still midnight before we pulled up at the ranch gate. The further south we had come, the nearer the misses were as deer jumped in, on, and by the highway. We were all a little weak kneed from the experience. I got out of the truck and spun the combination lock and opened the gate. Ken drove in and I locked the gate and got in the truck. We hadn't gone 100 yards when the biggest buck we had ever seen crossed the caliche road in front of us Ken exclaimed "Whoa boy, this is going to be a hunters paradise."

The road curved this way and that, up and down, and we finally went around a sharp curve and the head lights hit a butler building in a grove of mesquites. There was a windmill and tank beside it. I told Ken "That's the hunting lodge – pull up to the front door." I jumped out, went up to the door, and started fumbling with the lock. I yelled, turn off the truck lights and bring a flashlight. I didn't have my coat on and was freezing my fanny off – it was cold. Slim sidled up and shined the light on the lock and I got it open, went inside and turned on some lights. Next, I lit all the gas heaters I could find and put on a pot of coffee. Meanwhile, Ken and Slim were unloading our gear (basically clothes and guns). And the groceries we had stopped and bought in Junction. Slim turned on the T.V. – then turned it off and put a Willie Nelson tape in the tape player. Ken meantime had built a fire in the fireplace and each of us had done a walkthrough of the place. It really was two metal buildings, about 30 x 60 each, which they had put together in a T shape. One building contained the kitchen and the rest was a big open den area with a big fireplace at the end. The other building had a hallway down the center and five bedrooms on each side. We also located four bathrooms with showers. It was fully carpeted and by far the nicest deer camp we had ever seen. (Although since then I have had folks describe some others even nicer).

We sat down in some plush chairs in front of the fireplace, sipping our coffee and puffing on Marlboros and Ken said "This is sure enough top drawer." Slim replied "If it was any better we couldn't stand it" − I added "And the Sheriff wouldn't allow it." We had truly found deer hunters paradise. I drug out the map of the place and we each picked out an area we wanted to hunt the next day then went to bed and Willie sang us to sleep. We slept fast and were back up at 5 a.m. We were all so anxious to hunt that we just had coffee and some donuts and headed out in the dark with our flashlights. We had agreed to meet back at the "lodge" around noon and if anyone got lost or in trouble to fire 3 rapid shots. I was headed southwest, and Slim headed back down the road toward the front gate. (He remembered that huge buck). As I walked along I could hear deer crashing through the brush and hoofs clanking or rocks.

I was following a dim road through heavy brush and mesquites with clearing now and then. It was still dark but dawn was starting to break as I was looking for − an old barn. When I got to the barn there were some cows milling around and there was a small stack of hay they were munching on. The main doors were open on both ends of the barn so I went in and found a 5 gallon can with a lot of cigarette butts on the ground by it. I eased up and sat down and started looking down the hill through the back door. David had told me there was a tank and feeder about 75 yards down the hill from the barn. Sure enough, as it started to get light I could see the tank and several deer started to take shape at the feeder . I couldn't tell if I was seeing a big rack in the bunch or just imagining it. It finally got light enough that I was sure it wasn't my imagination – I could see real good through my rifle scope and there were three does and two bucks at that feeder – an 8 pointer and a real good 10 pointer. I was starting to get the shakes (buck fever). I had never taken a shot at a deer that big. While I was sitting there trying to collect myself I heard a shot off in the distance in the direction Ken had gone. I figured Ken had himself a trophy.

I finally calmed down and decided it was time to collect my trophy so I put the cross hairs on about where his heart should be and gently squeezed the trigger – K-Boom! He dropped like he had been pole axed and the rest of the deer scattered.

I walked down to where the buck lay and untied the length of rope I had tied around my waist and drug him over to a tree and tied the rope around his rack and threw it over a low limb and pulled him up – he was heavy and it took all my strength and 200 pounds to get him off the ground and strung up proper so I could field dress him. The job complete, I went over to the tank and washed up before I started back to the lodge. A big doe crossed the road ahead of me and when I saw her I threw up my gun and aimed at her – she stepped back into the brush but I caught a glimpse of another deer in my scope and instinctively put the cross hairs on him - and saw a big rack – and fired. He too dropped in his tracks. As I walked to him I thought, you idiot – you've used your two tags and the hunt is over for you. But when I got to the deer and examined him, I wasn't that disappointed cause he was another 10 pointer with a bigger and nicer rack than the other one.

I didn't have any more rope so I field dressed him as best I could on the ground and started on to the lodge – figuring I'd go there, clean up, and come back and get him with the pickup.

When I got in view of the lodge I could see smoke coming out of the chimney and knew someone had beat me back – turned out to be Ken. He already had a pot of coffee brewed and a platter of sausages fried, and biscuits baked. While I washed he scrambled some eggs and I came back to the kitchen and ate a heavy breakfast. Ken told me he had real nice 12 pointer strung up in a tree and I told him about my two. We were sitting at the table drinking coffee, smoking, and talking when we heard Boom!, Boom!, Boom!. Ken said, "Oh dern, Slims in trouble." We jumped up and rushed to my pickup and went bouncing down the road toward the front gate. We same upon Slim about 2/3 of the way to the gate, he was standing in the road looking dejected. We stopped, got out, and asked him "What's wrong."

He said, "I know I killed that monster buck that we saw last night but I can't find him." He went on to explain all the details and took us to the spot where the buck was standing when he shot. He swore that he knocked him down and we found both blood and hair on the ground to substantiate his story. He said that when he started to the buck after he shot he had to take a detour to get across a small creek and while he was out of sight of the deer it must have got up and run off.

We decided to each go in different directions to look for "sign" and see if we couldn't track the deer down. Ken and I had left our rifles back at the lodge so I went to my truck and got my .357 Mag pistol and strapped it on and got my .22 rifle which I took to Ken. We parted and went scouting in different directions. I found some blood on brush and on the ground and yelled "Over here." The blood was light colored and foamy and I knew we had problems – a long shot. They got there and examined the evidence and knew what I knew.

We decided that I would stay on the "sign" and try to establish the direction he was going and they would move out ahead and zig zag across the imagined trail – when in sight of me they would whistle and I would point the apparent direction. We started off and worked on our plan for about an hour – the brush was thick and we had probably traveled about two miles. We stopped to rest, smoke, and talk it over. Slim was starting to really get concerned but we told him we would look all day if necessary – it was about noon by then.

As we got ready to move out again Ken said "Is that a fence I see over yonder?" We looked in that direction and decided that it was. Ken said, "I'm going over there and walk that fence a ways" and left. In a few minutes he yelled, "Here he is deader than Santa Anna." We ran over to Ken and when Slim saw the huge deer he exclaimed "I told you that buy was a monster – Heck, he's big as a Brazos Riverboat." My how his mood had changed. And rightly so, it was a 14 point buck and the largest deer any of us had ever killed. We lifted him up and put his rack in the fence by a post and field dressed him. When we finished we realized we were nearly lost – I knew the direction of the pickup truck and knew we could follow the fence back to the front gate. Remembering the map (which I had left at the lodge) I also mentally calculated the direction of the lodge (I had navigation training in the Air Force) and also calculated it was closer than my truck.

I suggested we head for the lodge. They argued and said even if we get to the lodge, we'll still have to walk to get the truck. I said "Wrong – didn't you see that small building back of the lodge – there's an old army

Jeep in it that David said we could use." That settled the matter and we started breaking our way through the brush toward the lodge. In a little while I smelled the wood smoke from the fireplace and knew my calculations were correct sure enough, in a few minutes we popped out of the brush into the road – about 50 yards from the lodge. We went inside and cleaned up and Slim wolfed down the left over's – he was hungrier than a woodpecker with a sore pecker or so he said.

The sun was shining bright and it had warmed up considerable – so much that we decided we had better get our deer to a locker plant or else they might spoil. I found the keys to the Jeep and we cranked it up and headed for my truck. When we got to the truck, Slim took the Jeep and was going to the gate and drive the fence line to get his deer – Ken went with him and they would go pick up Ken's deer and meet me at the lodge. In the meantime, I would take the truck and go pick up my two deer.

After a while we met at the lodge, loaded all the deer in my truck, and headed for Del Rio. We had no trouble finding a locker plant and "deposited" them. We filled the gas tank, got a six pack, and a few groceries and headed back to the Double Eagle. We were all happy as a dog with two tails. This was, by far, the most productive deer hunt we had ever taken.

It was getting late when we went through the ranch gate so we decided not to hunt any more that day. We went on back to the lodge and started fixing supper. When we sat down to eat we heard Ring! Ring! Ring! Slim said "What's that?" Ken got up and went over to the wall and lifted the wall phone receiver and said "Hello?" Then he looked at me and said "It's for you." I got up and he handed me the phone. It was David calling to tell me to expect a "Guest" tomorrow. He said Archibald Van Peel, from New York, was coming down for a "Trophy" hunt.

David went on to explain how important it was for Archibald to have a good time and to get a nice trophy – he inferred that I might even shoot one for him if he failed. I recognized the name and knew that the New York Van Peels owned a lot of stock in David's Oil Company and they also supplied almost all of his drilling money. I promised David we would take good care of Mr. Van Peel. David said that he had also called the ranch owner, Mr. Ramirez, and told him – just so there would be no problems.

Slim and Ken sat there looking sort of puzzled and Slim asked "What the hell was that all about." I explained things to them and Slim said "Aw shucking" – we need Archibald like an armadillo needs an interstate highway." I said, fellers, you know what the rules were before we came down here. Since I've already got my limit, I'll look after Mr. Van Peel and you two continue to hunt. They grumbled till we finally went to bed. I told them I was going to sleep in next morning and drive over the ranch to look it over good around late morning.

The next morning I heard them rattling around in the kitchen and talking and then heard the door slam – so I rolled over and went back to sleep. I got up around 10 a.m. and fixed some breakfast, ate, smoked a cigarette, then got a fishing rod and a couple of lures. I had found in the closet, found the map, and got in my truck and started exploring the ranch. I saw lots of cows, deer, wild turkeys, and javlinna – also flushed several coveys of quail. This place was like a game preserve. I had my camera out, the windows rolled down, and was driving slow. After awhile I heard "Bill – hold it?" I stopped and Ken came trotting up. He had killed a deer (10 pointer) and a turkey and wanted me to pick them up – and we did. I always carry water in my truck so Ken took a big drink and also washed the blood off his hands. He wanted to ride around and see the ranch too. So we kept exploring. After a bit we came upon Slim and he wanted to ride – but standing in the bed so he could shoot a deer if he saw a good one. I came to the road that forked off to the old barn where I had killed my deer and drove slowly down it. Just as we got in sight of the barn, Slim pecked on the top of the cab (signal to stop) and I stopped – an instant later – K-Boom! Slim shot a deer that was standing up by the barn. When we drove up he said, in disgust "Doggone, this is only a six pointer."

I let Slim and Ken field dress the deer and I took the rod and reel and walked down to the tank and cast a lure out. It had no more hit the water than "Whoosh" – a big bass grabbed it. I played him a few minutes then drug him out on the bank. We weighed 5 or 6 pounds. I cast back in and in a few minutes landed a twin. The next couple of casts were unproductive but finally I hooked and landed a third bass – about the same size. I decided that was plenty for supper and quit. By the time I had the bass filleted, the deer was cleaned and loaded in the truck so we got in and continued to explore the ranch. Everywhere we drove we saw game. We flushed a covey of quail but they didn't fly far before they set down. Ken asked "You still have that .410 in the truck?" I said "Yes – it's in the toolbox and stopped and got it out – along with a hand full of shells. " Ken took the shotgun and slipped up to where the quail had landed and took a pot shot into them – killing 4. We turned down a road that got us headed toward the front gate and when we got there we drove in to the locker plant and deposited the deer when we got back to the ranch there was a yellow cab at the front gate.

When we pulled in to the gate, I got out to open the gate and the cab driver got out and trotted over and said "How do you get in to this place?" I said "Just follow us." He said, "I was about ready to dump this weirdo passenger right here and head back to San Antonio. He wouldn't pay me till he got properly situated at the hunting lodge." I said, "Follow us and your problem will be solved in a few minutes." I walked over to the cab, opened the door and introduced myself to Mr. Van Peel and told him we would be at the lodge in a few minutes. He was "pleased to meet you I'm sure and thank you." With that, I got in the truck and drove through the gate with the yellow cab right on my bumper. I stopped and Ken jumped out to close the gate.

When Ken got back in the truck Slim said "What does that feller look like – I couldn't get a good look at him." I said, "You will have that opportunity in a minute – but to answer your question, I would say he's about as strange as a brassier in a boys shower." Ken chimed in "Looks to me like he's about ten pickles short of a full barrel."

When we pulled up to the lodge we got out of the truck and the cab driver got out and opened the door for Archibald. Archibald reared back and took a deep breath and said "This is marvelous." He was decked out in an outfit more suited for a safari in a Africa and I'm sure some clerk at Abercrombie & Fitch had a field day outfitting him for this trip. We walked over to him and I introduced Ken and Slim who both said they were tickled to meet him and Archibald replied "My pleasure gentlemen." While we were getting the howdies taken care of the cab driver was hauling stuff from the trunk of the cab to the den area – it looked like Archibald brought aplenty.

After the driver finished unloading he stood there – waiting for payment. Archibald asked, "What is the toll my good man." The cab driver pretended to look at his meter and said "Two hundred twenty one dollars and fifty cents." Archibald pulled a roll of money big enough to choke a cow out of his pocket and peeled off three one hundred dollar bills and handed them to him with "Keep the change." The cabbie grinned, said thanks, and took off.

We all went inside and got Archibald "situated" in one of the bedrooms. While he was unpacking, we started to put supper together, we decided to surprise him with a wild game supper. We found some venison in the freezer so the menu included quail, turkey, venison, bass, green beans, mashed potatoes, gravy and cornbread (my specialty). When he came in to join us he really got excited at our bill of fare. He went back to the bedroom and returned with a bottle of Chivas Regal in one hand and Crown Royal in the other. Ken got some glasses and a tray of ice and we started toasting "Texas", "trophy deer", "wide open spaces", etc., etc. Archibald kind of reminded me of what I thought that Teddy Roosevelt would have been like.

By the time everything was cooked it had gotten dark outside and we had gotten almost drunk inside. Archibald kept saying "Bully" (guess that's why I thought Teddy Roosevelt), we literally had a feast and all of us had a good time. Before we went to bed I told Ken and Slim to not wake Archibald in the morning – just go on hunting. I said I would take him hunting after he woke up.

Next morning I woke up and smelled the coffee and bacon and heard laughing and loud talking. I went to the kitchen and all three were there. They said Archibald was the first one up. He was making the most noise also – telling about all these great hunts he had seen in movies, read about, etc. He uncased his rifle and showed it to us – it was a Weatherby – and a beautiful gun that cost more than all of our stuff – combined. Upon direct questioning, Archibald confessed that this was actually his first real hunt but concluded that he wasn't leaving until he had a "trophy." He had been quizzing Ken and Slim about deer hunting and had a general idea of what it was about. However, he was so fired up and eager I was afraid he might shoot a cow. So I gave him a lecture about not shooting cows. He wanted to know what they looked like so I described them. He still wasn't sure so I said "I'll take you to a place where the cows are and you can see them in person.

Ken and Slim got their guns and slipped out to go hunting and I stalled around a while – I really didn't want Archibald out there till it got light. As it was cracking first light Archibald and I got in my pick up and drove to the old barn. I stopped short of the barn and as we walked up to it, I pointed out the cows. He promised not to ever shoot a cow. We got to the barn and I let him sit on the can and told him where to watch for a deer. I figured they heard us talking and ran off but would return to the feeder or to water.

But the deer didn't return and Archibald was getting as jumpy as a hog in a packing plant. I eased back toward the front door to see if maybe there was a deer out in that direction and about that time I heard a loud K-Boom! I looked around in time to see Archibald jump up and run down the hill so I started running after him. He was running to claim his "trophy". But when he got to it this Mexican cowboy was sitting on it. Archibald yelled "That's my trophy deer! Get off it immediately." "Si Senior, you can have it, "The humble Mexican said – "But first let me remove my saddle and bridle."

CHAPTER 5

DON'T TAKE A DOCTOR HUNTING

Back in the Model A days, Sam Hopkins and Garrett Smiley had been planning a deer hunt all summer - summer of 1933. Things were kind of tough in Dallas that summer - depression and all - and they decided to invite Dr. Joshua Pritchett to go along on the hunt with them. Doc Pritchett had a Model A Ford you see and generally had cash money to spend besides. Get the point.

Sam had a cousin named Calvin Hopkins who had a ranch near Cherokee, San Saba County. The two or three dog-eared letters that Calvin wrote to Sam that summer and early fall told of a good deer crop that year and encouraged them to come hunting Matter of fact, conditions must have been extra good for Calvin told Sam that his wife, Sarah, was with child too.

As November drew nearer, Sam and Garrett grew more excited about the coming hunt. However, their spirits fell. when Doc informed them that he was afraid he couldn't get away - there was a flu epidemic developing in Dallas.

Lady Luck finally smiled on them - on Nov. 22 Doc drove over to Sam's house and told him to load up - the flu was whipped. Garrett lived next door so it didn't take long to load the Model A with rifles, boots, blankets, skillet, coffee pot, corn likker, etc. Doc, by force of habit, had even loaded his little black bag. (Doctors who make house calls in those days always carried the tools of their trade in a little black bag.) At first light the next day they got in the Model A and headed. southwest. It was a full two-day trip over rough roads and they arrived at Calvin's ranch about dark the second day.

Sam hadn't seen Calvin and Sarah in over three years so there was much back-slappin' and hugging before they finally sat down to the big supper which Sarah had prepared. During supper, Garrett embarrassed Sarah by asking if she had swallowed a watermelon seed that summer. So immediately after she cleaned the table and dishes she excused herself and went to bed. The men folk stayed up late, smokin', talkin', and nippin' at the corn likker which Sam produced from the Model A. Calvin told them of a big ole buck with a rockin-chair rack that he and some of the ranch hands had seen in the southwest corner of the ranch. The thought of that big buck was enough to convince the hunters that deer camp ought to be near the southwest corner of the ranch. Calvin agreed to lead them back to a good camping spot by a windmill come daylight. With that settled they all agreed to call it a night and hit the hay-literaly. The mattresses were filled with the stuff.

At daybreak Calvin went around and rustled everyone out of the hay. Doc was the hardest of get up since he had enjoyed the corn likker the most the night before. However, the smell of coffee brewin and bacon frying finally pulled him out of bed and into his boots-his kidneys encouraging the move as well.

Breakfast over and toileting complete, the hunters climbed into the Model A - all except Garrett whose task it was to "twist the tail" to get it started. Calvin in the meantime had saddled his horse and was already about a half-mile from the house before the cold natured car decided to start. They soon caught up with Calvin and drove slowly behind him. After crossing a couple of pastures three or four gates they finally arrived at the windmill- about 4 miles from the house, more or less.

Calvin stayed around for an hour or two and watched in amusement as the city folk fumed and fussed and finally got their tent and camp set up. Sam built a fire and started a pot of coffee and they drank coffee and listened to Calvin describe the lay of the land and how he would go about hunting for that big ole buck. They tried to convince him to stay for lunch but he was concerned for the misses and decided to, leave. He then told them he would come by each night to check on them. They planned to stay for four nights.

After Calvin left they were in a hurry to start hunting so they ate some cold biscuits and canned meat and washed it down with coffee. Each described where and how he was going to hunt that afternoon and agreed to be back to camp before dark. They also agreed on three shots for "emergency" signal (including getting lost) and further agreed that the first one back in camp would build a fire and cook supper. With all agreeing out of the way, they started huntin'. Sam went West, Doc went South, and Garrett headed East (with the idea of circling South himself toward the haunt of the big old buck.)

Late in the afternoon, near sundown, Garrett and Doc heard a gunshot to the West. Sam heard it, too. He fired it. He killed a nice, fat, four-point buck and was almost finished field-dressing it when Doc walked up. They cut a pole and tied the legs together and put the pole between the legs and were headed toward camp when Garrett arrived. It was already starting to get dark so Garrett agreed to "head for camp and start supper and they would take their time hauling the deer in. Garrett took the kidney, liver, and a piece of loin and headed for camp.

Doc and Sam could see and smell the campfire and smell the aroma of coffee boiling and venison broiling long before t.hey got to camp. They tied the deer carcus high on the windmill, washed up, and settled down to a supper fit for a king. They topped it off with cake which Sarah had baked the day before and gave to them that morning.

It wasn't till supper was long forgot ten and the corn likker was topping out a full day that Sam mentioned - "Wonder why Calvin hasn't showed up?" They thought up several reasons why not and had gotten off on their favorite subject - the big ole deer that they were going to shoot when they heard hoofbeats and the shout from Calvin - "Doc! Doc! Come quick - my wife is having the baby!"

DOC WAS RELUCTANT;.... SO THEY PUSHED HIM UPON THE HORSE!!

They all sprung into action and were trying to get the Model A started when Calvin galloped into camp. The Model A wouldn't fire up so Calvin told Doc to get on the saddle and ride to the house. Doc was reluctant to do so and Calvin climbed in the saddle and told the other two to push Doc up on the horse behind him. They finally got Doc aboard and as Calvin wheeled the horse around Doc yelled - "My bag, my bag, my little black bag." Calvin reined in for a second while Garrett scramble around in the Model A and finally came up with the little black bag and ran and handed it to Doc. That done, Calvin spurred the horse and let out a yell as they left in a cloud of dust. By the time they arrived at the ranch house, Doc had a bad case of the shakes - the corn likker and wild ride were almost too much for him. Calvin led him to the bedroom and Doc, with his little black bag in tow, entered. Doc promptly cleared Calvin out of the room and told him to get plenty of hot water and sheets. (Calvin started to feel a little more relieved after hearing instructions - even though Doc still had the shakes.)

While Calvin was stokin up the wood stove he heard the Model A drive up and Sam and Garrett hopped out and rushed into the house. While the three of them stood in the kitchen rather uneasily - Doc shouted -"Calvin, do you have a screwdriver?" Calvin yelled - "Yes sir". Doc said -"Fetch it quick". Calvin did as ordered and returned to the kitchen trembling. It didn't help matters when his wife started moaning, groaning, and yelling ever once in a while. Doc yelled again -"Calvin, bring a pair of pliers." Calvin replied - "Can't, lost mine the other day".

Doc responded - "Sam, go to the car and get the pliers under the seat and Calvin you go find a piece of bailing wire - and hurry, before it's too "late!" At the end of the last set of instructions Sarah let out a loud moan and Calvin almost fainted. Sam looked at Calvin and Garrett briefly, then yelled -"Doc, are you having trouble delivering that baby in there?" Doc replied - "Shucks no - I can't get the little black bag open, that's all!"

CHAPTER 6

RAPID COWS AND SPEEDIER CALVES

Much jest has been poked at, written about, and told of the country bumpkin's plight in the big city. Did you ever wonder what happens when the city slicker goes to the country?

Marvin City guy grew up in Brooklyn and spent his life there. He started a business and became a successful businessman. One December he came to Dallas to display his wares at Market Hall. He let his importance become known around the coffee shop and his obnoxious manner was beginning to wear on the locals.

One afternoon late he stopped at the coffee shop and was having a roll and coffee when he overheard a group at the next table talk about a deer hunt that they planned to take the next day. He recognized one of the voices as belonging to a customer and before the group of hunters realized what was happening - Marvin had joined the conversation and invited himself on the deer hunt.

Marvin really didn't know what deer hunting was all about. However, he had seen a movie once about a Safari in Africa so he had a general idea. The next morning he was at A & F (an exclusive sports shop) and they fixed him up with about $1,000 worth of things he would need for the hunt.

Late that afternoon, the group of hunters (who by now had recognized some possible sport in taking the city feller with them) picked him up in their Chevy Suburban at the Anatole. It was about 9:30 when they arrived at their deer camp on the Brandenberg ranch outside of Mason.

The next morning the hunters tried and tried to get Marvin up. He was so zipped up in his down filled-mountain A&F sleeping bag that they weren't having much success. Grady Jones kindly squawked on his varmint call a time or two and that did the trick. While the rest of the group had a big breakfast of ham and eggs, Marvin sat quietly in the corner of the tent drinking a coke and munchin a candy bar.

They loaded into the Suburban and headed out on the lease. They stopped at the first deer stand and helped Marvin up the tree and gave him instructions as to what to do after they got him settled they drove off giggling - each imagining what Marvin might do come daylight (shoot a cow, a goat. a horse: fall out of the tree; etc., etc.).

None of them were correct in their guess. It was cold up in that tree and as soon as it got light Marvin climbed down and headed back toward the warm sleeping bag. However, he wasn't sure of the direction of the camp but while in the tree he had heard familiar noises and seen lights to the North and that's the direction he took. After walking about 45 minutes he came upon a barn.

Homer Brandenburg, the rancher was in the barn at that very moment helping one of his cows deliver a calf. It was the first calf for this cow, and she was having trouble; and Homer literally had his hands full. He heard the city slicker yell, "Hello, there"; and he rushed to the door of the barn and saw him standing in the barn yard. Homer didn't recognize him but he was welcomed help for the "delivery" and Homer yelled for him to come into the barn.

Marvin, detecting urgency in Homer's voice, rushed into the barn. Homer rapidly explained what he wanted the stranger to do - "Grab the calf by the ears and pull hard"; and Homer immediately shoved his hand and arm up the cows "delivery device" and started helping her with the birth. After several minutes of cussing, sweating, and swearing, the delivery was complete and healthy calf let out a bleat and the cow a grateful moo.

Homer started walking toward the house followed by the befuddled city slicker. He stopped at the back porch and washed up, pitched out the bloody, soapy water, and refilled the wash pan for Marvin to do the same.

After they were cleaned up, Homer went into the house and poured each a glass of beer and came back out with the glasses in hand. They went over to a bench, sat down, and got acquainted. Homer didn't like the "cocky" and "smart aleck" manner of the stranger, but he was grateful that he had come along when he did; otherwise, he probably would have lost the calf and maybe the cow too. Marvin asked several "stupid" questions about the ranch which Homer answered in a puzzled manner.

After Marvin had rested and got his energy back, he said that he must head back to the deer camp. Homer offered to hitch up his horse and take him; but Marvin cast one frightened look toward the horse and declined - said he enjoyed walking.

Homer walked Marvin to the pasture gate and painted to the windmill near their deer camp. Marvin started to leave but stopped after taking a few steps, turned to Homer and said, "There was something. else I meant to ask". Homer said, "What?" Marvin, city slicker, asked, "Just how fast was that little cow running when he ran into the rear end of that big cow?"

B. BIRD HUNTING

Although the most popular form of hunting in Texas is deer hunting, I have always been partial to quail hunting. However, you don't call if "quail" hunting if you're a veteran hunter - it's just plain ole "bird hunting." Bird hunting can also include hunting for dove, pheasant, or most any bird that flies - except duck (which is "duck hunting").

The secret to successful bird hunting is a good bird dog - and of course, a hunting lease with several covey of quail on it. There are two types of quail in the state - the Bob White which ranges throughout east Texas, North, South, and Central Texas and the so called "Mexican quail" in the west Texas that run like pool cue balls on the ground , and won't hardly "Hold" for a point - it's difficult to get the little critters to fly. I expect that most of them that are killed are blasted while they are on the ground.

There are several breeds of bird dogs including pointers, setters, and spaniels. I've hunted behind good dogs of all three breeds but year in and year out - you can't beat a good pointer.

Another important ingredient for a successful bird hunt is a good shotgun - and the ability to use it. You must be able to get off multiple shots if you expect to get any meat to eat. Therefore, the most popular bird guns are automatics, pumps, and double barrels. Probably the most popular is a 12 gauge automatic but my favorite has always been a 20 gauge Remington pump. I've already worn mine out three times but I have a good friend who is a gunsmith that has re-barreled and rebuilt it for me.

Bird hunters are a peculiar lot - a different breed of cat. Don't ever criticize or mistreat one of their dogs - unless you want a load of bird shot in the hind end.

CHAPTER 7

REMINSCIENCE OF A BIRD HUNTER

Back in the 60's I helped a new client structure a substantial transaction that allowed him to make and keep a large amount of money. He was grateful of course. and as I got to know him better we learned that each of us had the same great passion - bird hunting.

He purchased a ranch in Jack County near Jermyn with a part of his money and until he passed away about a dozen years later I had a place to quail hunt anytime I felt like it and a hunting companion who was always ready and eager to go. The last couple of years of his life he couldn't do much walking, but he would go nevertheless and stay in the pickup. Anytime that I could drive the truck near the dogs on point he would get out and pop a cap or two. He would always say "Boy - go find the singles and I'll fetch the dead birds", He would get back in the truck and pop the top on a can' of beer and watch as the dogs and I hunted up the singles and then moved on out to locate another covey.

I'll call him Joe Smith for the purposes of this story. he was about thirty years my senior and our relationship was akin to father/son and I dearly loved that old man. He taught me a lot about bird hunting and life in general - particularly people. He had grown up in Jack County and had many relatives in that part of Texas, although he had spent all his adult life in Dallas.

The ranch he bought contained a section (640 acres) and was run down. The old frame house hadn't been occupied for a few years, the tanks were silted up or leaked. and the barn was almost beyond repair. I went out with him many weekends that first summer and helped with the renovation. He also bought an old tractor and plow and we planted some patches of milo and wheat around the place - purely for feed for the quail. He put a few old cows on the place just to make it a legitimate ranching operation. by the first winter, we had the old house livable, but not luxurious. (It didn't have a TV). Heat was supplied by a large wood burning stove in the front room and a kerosene gas heater in the kitchen.

Joe owned a young Brittany Spaniel (named "Mutt") and I had a liver colored pointer named Sissy which we hunted with that first year. The birds were plentiful that season and we never got off his place to hunt - didn't need to. By the middle of the season we had about ten coveys located and could always find all we needed. We went to the ranch practically every weekend during hunting season (eleven or twelve weekends) and hunted each time we went out. Sometimes he would stay a day or two extra but I would have to get on back to my job in Dallas. I would leave old Sis with him. Gradually it sort of evolved that we located a fellow in Jacksboro who boarded and trained bird dogs and we started leaving our dogs with him during the week and finally permanently. We also bought some "partnership" bird dogs over the years which we boarded with the trainer.

One of the "partnerships" dogs we owned was an old gyp which we called Nell- and she was still a fine hunter. She ranged out and found the birds first most of the time. However, she had one fault and if you or one of the other dogs didn't beat her to a downed bird, she would gobble it down like it was a can of Alpo. One time we had a banker from Wichita Falls join us for a weekend of bird hunting. He was a camera nut as well as a hunter and he had a camera strapped around his neck that morning as we took to the field. We had kind of hinted to Mr. Banker that if he happened to shoot a bird in front of old Nell he should command "Whoa!" and hold her while they looked for the dead bird, or better yet-tie her and let one of the other dogs search for "dead bird". Anyway, he didn't pay much attention to us and by mid morning the inevitable happened. Old Nell pointed a single and he was the closest to her so he walked over to her and kicked it up and shot it. He immediately unslung his camera as he walked toward the cripple and was busily taking snapshots of old Nell as she maneuvered through the tall grass trying to catch the crippled bird. Joe and I were watching to see what was going to happen. Directly we heard Mr. Banker exclaim loud "God Almighty - look at this". We didn't get over to him soon enough to see what "this" was, but he sent us a photograph later of what he had witnessed. There was old Neill smiling up at him with a quail leg and foot protruding from each side of her mouth.

"THERE WAS OLD NEILL SMILING UP AT HIM WITH A QUAIL LEG & FOOT PROTRUDING FROM HER MOUTH."

Young dogs could also be trouble at times - so could cows. And the two of them just didn't mix. A couple of seasons we ended up with young dogs that were "started" on quail. That meant they knew what quail smelled like and would trail them on the ground. point them occasionally. but flush them mostly and chase after them when they flew. Young dogs had to chase every rabbit that jumped up - deer. too - and would invariably locate a skunk and stir him up if there was one around. It was always a problem if we happened on to the cows. The young dogs would run up to them and bark and one or two of the old cows would butt at them and we usual1y ended with a three ring circus. I'm sure that bunch of old cows had devious minds for when they would finally decide to run off. often we yelled and cussed at the dogs a few times - they invariably ran to precisely the cover we planned to work and would spend the next hours staying about one hundred fifty yards ahead of us - going from one .area we intended to hunt to the next - completely ruining our hunt. I'm sure Joe was on the verge of slaughtering his herd more than once - I know I was.

One night we were sitting by the wood stove telling about the troubles we had that day with those two knot headed young pointers. Old Joe had stayed at the house after a frustrating morning round but I had taken the two young dogs back out after lunch and took them on a big sweep around the place and hunted them till dark. I had been tough on them but felt they needed it if we were going to get any decent hunting in the balance of the season. When I brought them in that night they were so tired they hardly touched the big pan of dog food in the pen but elected to crawl in their nice insulated dog house and literally hit the hay. Anyway. as I was saying. we were sitting by the nice warm fire sipping some juice. when the young bird dogs started barking and carrying on down in the dog pen by the barn. It was cold outside and old Joe was already dressed for bed. I had taken my boots off but was still dressed so I "volunteered" to check on the dogs. I slipped my boots on, put on a coat, got a flashlight, and headed for the dog pen.

When I got close to the dog pen I spotted these two fiery eyes glowing in the light — almost at eye level. I didn't have a gun with me but proceeded on anyway. I didn't figure there were many things out any tougher than I was - gun or no gun - so I kept walking. Finally I got close enough to see what was going on. There was a big coon perched on the comer fence post and the dog food was scattered all over the dog pen — the two young dogs were standing in the middle - of the dog pen, looking up at the coon and barking their fool heads off. I decided to settle the standoff real quick so I doubled up my fist, walked over to the fence post, and knocked the old coon right into the middle of the dog pen with the two young dogs. The result was the loudest but shortest coon fight in history. Before you could say Jack Spratt the old coon had slapped both dogs silly and they were back inside the dog house and he was helping himself to the dog food. I watched him for a minute and went on back to the house When I got back to the wood stove old Joe said "What the heck was going on out there? I replied, "aw nothing, the dogs were just fighting over the dog food".

THE DOGS WERE INSIDE THE HOUSE... AND HE WAS HELPING HIMSELF TO THE DOG FOOD.

The quail population would vary from year to year. Some years, there seemed to be a quail under every weed and bush. Other years, you would have to hunt the place real hard just to find one small covey. The biologists have explained all the reasons for this phenomenon—rainy spring, dry spring, short life cycles, etc, etc. All I know is that those years when there were hardly any birds we would end up "mooching" permission to hunt on all of Joe's cousins, uncles, nephews, etc. property in Jack and Montague Counties. Those years, we ended up spending a lot of what would otherwise have been hunting time-visiting with his relatives. After all, it isn't proper to drive out to relatives property — hunt — and leave — without at least stopping for a visit, and many of those "visits" took up a half a day. I didn't particularly care for all that much visiting so we ended up "leasing" a couple of ranches owned by non-relatives. That worked out much better.

Some years; there seemed to be a quail under every weed and bush!

Except for this one ranch we leased. It didn't cost much and was large - around 1,800 acres as I recall. However, it had been thoroughly overgrazed and the only decent cover was a hillside on the back of it that had a briar thicket and scrub oak so thick the old cows couldn't get through it. And you know where what few birds there were on the place all decided to live -you got it! That in itself was a serious problem but the real problem was the neighbor across that fence line. He didn't allow hunting at all on his property -- none, no exceptions, stay the heck off my place, etc. And old Leroy (not his real name) wasn't one to trifle with. He had been a lineman for T.C.U. and was one big rancher.

His house was about half mile from that fence line and more often than not he would pull up in his blue Ford pick-up on his side of the fence every time we fired a few shots. He and Joe had known each other for years - matter of fact, they were about the same age and had been rival suitors for one of the local belles when they were young men. We would invariably end up "shooting the breeze" with Leroy for a while. He would never accept our offer of a beer but we would sip one anyway as we "visited," he would always part with - "I heard shooting and thought I' d better come check - You all know I don't allow any hunting on my property."

Before that season was over what few birds there were on the lease caught on - to the "set up". The minute we started - hitting the briars and brush on the lease, they would flush wild and fly across the fence to Leroy's sanctuary.

A couple of hunts like that was all I could stand The next time we hunted I had old Joe keep the dogs leashed while I circle the brush, crawled through the fence, and stationed myself on the properly line (on Leroy's side however) - waiting in ambush. Joe turned the dogs loose and in less than five minutes I heard the whirr of quail wings as the birds flushed out of the briars and headed for Leroy's. I slipped off the safety and nailed two of them as they passed over. As I started looking for the dead birds I caught a glimpse of blue and I knew Leroy was on his way. I found one bird and was on my hands and knees - frantically looking for the second and trying to stay out of Leroy's sight as he approached I finally found the bird and had crawled through the fence when he drove up. He was madder than a hornet but didn't say much or accuse me of trespassing. However, our "visit" that morning was short and his parting shot was" I ever catch a hunter crawling around on my property. I'm going to kick his a-- up between his shoulder blades". He got into his blue pickup and as he drove off I saw a pair of binoculars hanging on his gun rack. As Joe and I left the lease heading back to his ranch 1 said "You know, Joe, I don't see any reason to come back here and hunt anymore - there aren't any birds". Joe winked and said "You're right

boy". And besides that, a feller could get hurt crawling around on it."
And we never went back.

Weather could affect your hunting, too. I've seen it get so warm during "Indian, Summer" (in December) that the rattlesnakes would un-hibernate and crawl out and lay in the sun, particularly on the limestone ledges that dot the countryside. You hunted in short sleeved shirts and watched where you stepped at the other extreme, I've been out on the back side of the place hunting in a light coat and have a Blue Northern come through and come very near to freezing to death before I could get back to the house and get a fire going. I remember one week end when it started sleeting and spitting snow before we ever got to the ranch on Friday night. By the time we unloaded dogs, groceries, etc. it was sleeting so bad that you couldn't see fifteen feet ahead of you. We soon had the fire going (simple - throw some small sticks in first, cover with larger chunks of mesquite douse with diesel. and throw a match in), and a couple of cans of soup warming. Soon we were cozy and comfortable and the weather didn't bother us. We went to bed and it was still sleeting and was spitting snow when we got up the next morning. When I looked outside I guarantee I thought I had been kidnapped and transported to Siberia. It was one of the bleakest scenes I had ever seen - everything was covered with ice and sleet. Joe looked it over and decided he wasn't going hunting in that mess and went back to bed.

Once I wake up it is nearly impossible for me to go back to sleep after daylight so I put on a pot of coffee, built a fire, and eventually cooked and ate breakfast. I took some table scraps to the dogs and checked on them. They were fine, and old Mutt (who was about eight at the time) seemed even friskier than usual. I fretted around the house until almost noon - trying to decide, should I go hunting in all' that sleet and ice or shouldn't I?   I guess poor judgment finally got the best of me for I bundled up good, laced on my boots, got my gun and old Mutt, and headed across the barn lot - crunch. crunching. as I walked over that ice and sleet. Mutt ran off and did number one and number two scratched in the sleet and was eager to go. We walked and walked and Mutt tried his best to find birds but couldn't, We went to all the areas where we had found quail the previous weekend but none could be found - anywhere. It was weird. By now Mutt was getting tired. his feet were cut and bleeding. and he was giving me that look - "What are we doing out here you idiot - I want to crawl back into my warm bed." About that time it started snowing so we headed back toward the house. On the way back we took a short cut through a patch of woods that had a dry creek down through the middle of them. Normally we never hunted the woods except when a flushed covey would fly into them. Mutt had quit hunting and was walking along with me. Suddenly, he got real "birdy" and tip toed over toward the creek bank and froze on - point I didn't believe him and told him so as I walked over to him - birds started flying out of some brush under that creek bank and continued-to come out of there. I emptied my sixteen gauge pump, reloaded, emptied it again. reloaded. and emptied it at least one more time before the birds quit flying out of there. I am satisfied there were between seventy and one hundred quail congregated in that one space. We picked up nine dead birds and headed on to the ranch house. I fed Mutt and put him to bed and cleaned the birds. I was afraid to tell Joe what had happened - fearful that he wouldn't believe me and would laugh at my wild story. When I washed the birds and, placed them in the refrigerator. Joe said "Where did you get those birds? You must have hunted the woods - they all congregate along that creek for protection when the weather gets this bad". With that statement I proceeded then to tell Joe what I had experienced.

SUDDENLY...MUTT GOT REAL BIRDY.

One year, I had missed about half the weekends of hunting season because of demands of my job and before I realized it, February was there and it was the last week end of quail season. I was determined to hunt that last week end despite the fact that my wife forced me to take her to a formal dinner dance on Friday. I went home after work Friday and snuck my gear and hunting clothes in the trunk of the car while my wife wasn't looking and then got ready for the dinner dance. I was decked out in black, formal attire and all slicked up. We went to the dinner-dance and were having a real good time with our friends and with the refreshments. I finally looked at my watch which showed it was near midnight and I suddenly remembered I had about a two hour drive ahead of me if I was going to go hunting - which I was. The orchestra finally stopped playing and the party was over, however, on the way home my wife insisted that we stop at a Denny's and have some coffee and eggs to sober me up some. We did and it was about 1:30 am. when I finally got her home, kissed her good night, and told her I was going bird hunting. I left her fussing at me as I got back in the car and pulled out, headed for the ranch. I had driven about an hour and happened to look at the fuel gauge - it was on E and I was out in the middle of nowhere on a farm to market road and it was about 20° outside. I figured that I was about fifteen miles from Bridgeport so I crossed my fingers and kept driving. I coasted into Bridgeport' about 3:00 A.M. and it was sound asleep. Absolutely nothing was open but I saw a light in a side window of the city hall building and decided to see who was up. I parked the car and walked to the door and entered. There was a policeman sitting behind a desk, drinking coffee and, reading a magazine. I sure wish I' d had a camera and got a picture of his expression as he looked up and saw a fellow coming through the door - dressed in a tuxedo and with a silly grin, on his face. I said "Hidey - do you know where a feller could get some gasoline in this town?" He stared at me for a long time and finally said- "Buddy, I'm going to lock you up - you're drunk." I said "Naw, I'm sober as a judge- all I need is a couple of gallons of gas so I can get to the ranch." There followed a three-or four minute conversation, rather. a question and answer session. I had to explain the tuxedo of course, etc. etc. Finally he asked - "Where did you say you were going?" Then I said the magic words "Going bird hunting." He was a bird hunter himself and became sympathetic to my predicament. He got a key ring off the wall and instructed me to follow him in my car. I got back in my car and cranked it up and started to follow the police car. However, I hadn't gone two blocks when my car quit running- completely dry, I flashed my lights and he circled back. I told him it was completely out of gas so he gave me the directions to the filling station and then pushed me there with the police car. He opened the station, turned on the gas pumps, and I put in ten dollars worth of gas. I paid him, gave him my business card, and told him to look me up the next time he was in Dallas - I wanted to buy him a big steak. With the fuel gauge now past one half I was in great spirits as I continued west. In about an hour I pulled into the front yard at the ranch house, got the key from under the rock. and let myself inside. I didn't want to wake Joe so I decided not to turn on any lights but to feel my way to the bed in "my" bedroom, slip off my shoes, and catch a couple of hours of sleep before daylight. I know the house well enough that I had no problem getting to the bed despite the fact that it was pitch dark inside. I took off my shoes, pulled back the covers, and crawled into a warm bed which was already occupied by two men - the men who had gone out Friday with Joe that I didn't know about. Anyway, what followed was another vignette that should have been captured on film. The bed was next to the wall and the light switch was about ten feet from the bed. Both men woke up and started yelling and struggling to climb out of the bed - they had to climb over me to do so. All the commotion woke Joe up and the lights came on finally - Joe was standing in the door in his night shirt - one hand on the light switch and holding a shotgun in the other. When he saw me rise up out of the bed, throw back the covers and expose my tuxedo and silly grin - he came unglued. I never saw him laugh so hard in my life. It took a little explaining before the other two fellers saw the humor in it.

I got up, built a fire, put on a pot of coffee, and was soon joined by the others. We drank coffee and talked till daylight. Joe said - "Bout time we went bird huntin - Bill, are you going to change clothes or go like you are?" (I still had on the tuxedo and bow tie). Man, them were the good old days!

CHAPTER 8

THREE IMMORTAL TEXAS BIRD DOGS

It was late winter and the boys were huddled around the gas heater at the domino parlor in Breckinridge, Stephens County, Texas and someone commented that it had been a good season for the bird (quail) hunters. Everyone agreed and the talk drifted to bird dogs. It seemed that everyone there had, at one time or another, owned a prize-winning bird dog.

Here are the three dogs that stood above all the rest which makes them immortal in my mind.

"OLE ABE"

Abe

Pullet Elson told of a dog he once owned, a white and black freckle-spotted setter name Abe, that was the most honest dog on the point he ever knew. He said the dog never lied. One time he remembered, they had been hunting nearly all day and old Able pointed. They moved in behind him and a bird flew out low and fast and he and his hunting companion were just barely able to snap off a shot at the bird as it went over a hill. They went and looked for the bird but never found it. After they had made a big circle and were headed back to the pick-up truck, they passed near the spot where the bird crossed the hill and ole Abe pointed-straight into a stock tank. The hunting companion really ribbed Pullet about a bird dog that didn't know the difference between a fish and a bird. Pullet took all the ribbing he could stand and broke off a tree branch and was about to give ole Abe whipping when a big bass floated to the surface near the edge of the tank. Pullet took the tree branch and used it to pull the bass to the bank where he caught it with his hand and lifted it out of the water. The bass was so rounded that he decided to cut him open. When he did, the dead quail fell to the ground. As always, ole Able had told the truth.

Albert E.

Joe Bob Ausenbaugh told of the smartest dog he ever heard of. He claimed that he once owned a liver-spotted German shorthair pointer named Albert E. who was so smart that he would count the birds he had pointed and would look around at you when you walked up to shoot and wink once for each bird he was holding with the point. That way, you knew whether to get ready for a covey rise or just a single or pair.

By then, it was getting pretty deep in the domino parlor and the boys were starting to snicker and wink at one another. Old Judge Coffey cleared his throat and said, "Boys, that's the truth." One time Joe Bob took me bird hunting on the Davis place and the first time Albert E. pointed, we walked up behind him and he looked around and winked at us nine times. Joe Bob told me to be ready for a covey of nine birds to fly up-and they did. I counted exactly nine birds. Every time he found a single, he only winked once. A northern blew in that afternoon and it started to sleet. We headed back to the Model A and Albert E. pointed in a dry creek that had some brush and bushes in it. When we walked up behind Albert E. he was so nervous he was quivering. He sneaked over to the edge of the creek and picked up a dead tree limb and was shaking it furiously. I asked Joe Bob what was going on. Joe Bob said, "There are so many birds in here that you can't shake a stick at them." And there were--birds flew out of that creek for five minutes. That was some smart bird dog.

HOLY COW! MY DAWG!

OLE CONSTITUTION

Constitution

Jeff Davis told of a bird dog he once owned that would not leave a point. He was a lemon-spotted pointer named Constitution. Jeff claimed that if you were hunting with ole Constitution and he didn't circle by-- you had better start looking for him. He was on point and would not break it. He said that ole Constitution was the best dog he ever owned and that his untimely demise nearly broke his heart. There was a long silence and it was obvious that the boys wanted to hear about the fate of ole Constitution.

Jeff said that when Constitution was five years old he loaned him to his brother-In-law who lived In Jacksboro. His brother-in-law had invited some bankers on a bird hunt and he needed an extra dog. The dog was not returned when he was promised and his brother-in-law called several times with one excuse or another as to why he needed to keep him. Jeff was getting suspicious but every time he mentioned it, his wife lit into him and he let the matter drop. The winter passed, then spring, then summer. On July 4th they went to Jacksboro for a family gathering and Jeff confronted his brother-In-law face to face and demanded the return of ole Constitution. His brother-In-law confessed that he had lost the dog. He said that the bankers were in a hurry to get home and he called and called for ole Constitution but he never came. He claimed they spread out and looked hard for him before they left but he was nowhere In sight. He even went back the next day and called and called and looked and looked but couldn't find him.

Jeff demanded that his brother-in-law take him to the ranch where they had been hunting when Constitution disappeared. They went out there and walked the pastures. They came upon a briar patch and glimpsed something white In It. When they got close and parted the briars, there stood a Skelton of a bird dog--still on a staunch point.

CHAPTER 9

BIRD DOGS ARE FOREVER

If you have never raised a bird dog from a pup, trained and taken care of it, and watched it retrieve the first bird ever shot over it, then you may not fully appreciate this story. A bond develops between man and dog that I can't fully explain with mere words.

Orville Qua was a bird hunter and had been all his life. He grew up on a ranch south of Brady and always had fine birddogs. However, for the past five years he had two bird dogs that were his all time favorites. They worked better as a pair than any he had ever owned and he loved them-almost as much as his love for his wife. (She would swear more-particularly in December and January.)

Orville didn't deer hunt and he always suffered through deer season knowing full well that conditions were ideal at that time for bird hunting. However, he was patient and knew his time would come when the deer hunters cleared out.

The first day of bird season finally arrived on a Saturday but Orville got tied up with some ranch chores and didn't get to go. Sunday morning he was up at the crack of dawn and ready to go. A rancher friend north of town had talked him into coming up to his ranch for a hunt.(The friend had lots of birds, but no dogs.)

When Orville drove up In front of the house, his friend opened the door and headed for the pick-up-gun in hand. He gave Orville directions to the East pasture, suggesting they start the hunt where he had jumped six covey the day before.

They hadn't much more than stopped the truck, got out, opened the dog cage, and lit a cigarette when his friend yelled- "Point!" Orville looked out into the pasture at the dog on point and said-"Naw - B.M. - all dogs do that before they get serious about hunting." They had a good laugh and started walking.

Inside the first half mile the dogs did get serious and pointed two covey. They were both shooting good and they had seven birds and were In high spirits on that crisp winter morning.

However, when they got to the end of the pasture they had to cross a farm-to-market blacktop road to get into the next pasture which they planned to hunt. Disaster struck unexpectedly as they approached the blacktop, the two bird dogs were already out on the pavement and a car was coming at about 75 mph. Orville had just got his whistle to his lips when the car hit both dogs - killing them instantly-and continued down the road. Orville rushed to the broken bodies and clutched them in his arms-tears flowing freely down his cheeks. His rancher friend decided the best thing to do was to leave Orville with his two bird dogs while he walked back and got Orville's pick-up for him.

He got the truck and drove it to a gap gate and up on the blacktop road and down to where Orville was kneeling by the two dogs. Not a word was said as Orville gently placed the dogs in the bed of the pick-up; got in, and they drove off, Orville appeared to be in shock as he stopped and let his rancher friend out of the truck.

"ORVILLE HAD JUST GOT HIS WHISTLE TO HIS LIPS...... WHEN THE CAR HIT BOTH DOGS."

Orville had to drive right through Brady on his way home. As he was going through town he passed Ira Jones Taxidermy Shop. Almost in a trance, he pulled up at the shop and gently laid both dogs on the porch. He had forgotten it was Sunday so he just left the dogs lay and scrawled his name and phone number on a piece of cardboard and left it laying by the dogs. (This really wasn't necessary since nearly everyone in Brady, Ira included, would recognize the two liver spotted pointers.)

Monday morning Orville's phone rang. It was Ira calling from his shop. After expressing his condolences. Ira, not knowing whether Orville wanted the dogs stuffed or what. asked "Orville. did you want these two bird dogs mounted?"

Orville said. "Naw, Ira. just stand them side by side as they were brothers."

CHAPTER 10

THE AUTOMOTIC PUMP SHOTGUN

In not too many years past, the First Monday of each month was trading day in the country. Farmers and others gathered from miles around at the local county seat for a day of swapping.

Everything was traded--livestock, guns, hunting dogs, watches, and pocket knives being the predominate items exchanged.

An expert at tradin' might arrive in the morning with no more than a Barlow knife and after a few shrewd trades might ride home that night with a horse and saddle and leading a milk cow. My granddad was such a trader, and he relayed this story to me.

Granddad had swapped for a double-barreled shotgun the previous month; and to his dismay--he discovered that he had acquired a "bird gun." The reason he discovered it was a "bird gun" was that when he tried to shoot it at a rabbit--it wouldn't fire. After some research, he found out that the springs on the firing pins were broken so that the gun barrel had to be raised up for the firing pins to function. it would have been a minor repair job for a gunsmith; but Granddad was too proud--and tight--to have it fixed. Instead, he decided to "swap it off" on the next trading day.

Therefore, the next First Monday found Granddad and the "bird gun" at the Van Zandt county seat shopping around for a turkey. Granddad soon found out that the feller who had swapped the gun to him the month before had already been telling everyone how he had skinned Granddad, and practically everyone that Granddad met just who-whoed when he offered to swap the "bird gun" to them. By late afternoon Granddad was rather dejected and about to resign himself to the fact that for once in his life--he had been so skinned on a trade that he couldn't even trade off what he had traded for.

But, alas! Fate finally smiled upon him about sundown. He ran into Paddle foot Todd, the village Idiot; and Paddle foot had a gun that he was willing to swap. Granddad asked Paddle foot what kind of a gun it was that he was willing to swap for the "bird gun "(As Granddad truthfully described his double-barrel). Paddle foot said his was an "automatic pump." By now Granddad was really feeling smug--he had a sucker at last. He could tell that ·what Paddle foot had was a nice, Winchester, 12-gauge, pump shotgun; and any fool that knew anything about guns knew that there wasn't any such thing as an automatic pump.

Normally, In a gun swap the- two parties would walk out to a field near town and test each other's gun by firing them. However, since Granddad knew his gun wouldn't fire unless it was painted up, he was afraid that Paddle foot might try to shoot at a stick or post and discover the flaw. Therefore, Granddad suggested that since it was going to get

dark soon and since he had to drive his buggy about ten miles and then

feed and milk, they swap without the normal test firing.

SHE'S LIKE BRAND NEW!

Paddle foot allowed as how Granddad had a good point--however, he

needed a little change to buy some coffee, salt, etc; so if Granddad was

willing to pay $2 to boot--he would swap.

Granddad, smiling inwardly, knew he really had outfoxed Paddiefoot;

so he wasted little time In digging $2 out of his overalls and swapping.

That night, he could hardly wait to get inside the farmhouse to tell

grandma and the children what a good trade he had made for the "bird gun." The whole family, being fairly familiar with guns, really got a big laugh out of Granddad's telling about the trade--particularly about Paddle Foot's description of the Winchester as an "automatic" pump. That had to be about the funniest thing they had heard for months. Granddad went to bed that night feeling mighty proud of himself.

Next morning, after breakfast, my Uncle Forest wanted to try out the new shotgun before he went to school. Granddad got a handful of shells and his new Winchester shotgun, and they went outside and loaded the gun. Granddad handed the gun to Uncle Forest and told him to shoot it a couple of times.

As Uncle Forest tells it, "I pulled the trigger and she fired--BANG-- then I pumped her once and she went BANG again--except that time I didn't pull the trigger. I handed it to Paw, and he did the same thing.

Granddad then said, "Well, I'll be Dadgone! It is an automatic pump.

C. COON HUNTING

Coon hunting is like bird hunting in that you must have a good dog to do it right. But there the similarity ends. Coon hunting is done at night and generally you have a "Pack" of coon hounds that "trail" the coon and eventually chase it up a tree. They bark "treed" and the hunters go to them and try to get the coon out of the tree so they can watch a good coon and dog fight.

There are several breeds of hounds that are used for coon hunting - black and tan, redbone, bluetick, walker (best for fox hunting though) and plott (really - a bear dog.) I've also hunted with many Heinz 57 dogs that were fair coon dogs.

The best coon hunting is done on cold, damp, and drizzly winter nights - in other words, miserable weather.

It don't hurt to be a drunkard if you're going to do much coon hunting.

CHAPTER 11

A TALE OF CHASING THE MASKED "MIDNIGHT BANDIT"

"Shine your light up that hickory tree, boy." "Not the one Rebel is barking up-the hickory tree." I opened the value on my carbide lamp a notch or two more and followed the "Ole Feller's" Instructions. "Hot damn-look up there -three of em," shouted Royal Goodcare. Yeah said the Ole Feller, I could tell the way that Belle and Roosevelt were actin that we had more than one coon up a tree.

The Ole Feller .continued, "Royal, · catch a hold of Rebel and hold him and I'll hold Belle and Roosevelt while the boy climbs that scaly bark hickory tree and shakes them coon out of there-we're going to have us a show."

We had now reached the part of the coon hunt that I dreaded-the "show" part. To this day I don't know if I played a member of the supporting cast or the main character In the "show"-but I strongly suspect the latter.

The "show" consisted of me climbing the tree and somehow shaking or poking the coon out of it so that he fell to the ground where he was immediately pounced upon by two or three angry blue tick hounds bent upon shaking the daylights out of him. Sounds simple enough, right? Wrong!!

To begin with, the raccoon is an excellent tree climber whereas I was only so-so- even in the day time, in summer. We always hunted coons in the winter, at night, when· the temperature was always below freezing.

Part of our standard equipment was "hip boots" since we invariably hunted near water. My carbide light had a 10 inch reflector and I could not wear it (on my cap) while climbing. My handicaps therefore were (1) bulky winter clothing, (2) hip boots, and (3) no light; and I was opposing an "expert" In the tree tops.

Anyway, that's part of the way I earned my right to go along on the "coon " hunt" so up the tree I headed. I had long since learned that the coon critters were very unpredictable. Generally, the young ones would go out on a limb and I could shake It till they fell out. The old "boar coons" were a different story.

Sometimes they would come down the trunk to meet me-rarin' to fight. I have literally knocked a couple of them out of the tree with my fist-and I've also been run out of a tree myself by a real ornery one. It turned out this night that there were three young coons which I was able to shake out with little difficulty-the dogs caught one of them but the other two got away-for a while. Old Rebel trailed one of them up and treed it again but it was the den tree so we left him in the woods for another hunt.

It was getting late-past midnight, and the Ole Feller decided it was time to go home. He and Royal had to work at the coal mines the next day and I had school. We caught the dogs and headed for the pickup truck for the rough ride home.

They had been logging these woods some and the dirt roads were full of deep ruts-they were frozen solid so there was no danger of getting stuck. After we had gone away and the truck's heater had thawed us out I turned on the radio to WSM and we rode in silence and listened to Roy Acuff sing about the "Great Speckled Dove" or "Night Train to Memphis" as we rode home.

We were at our farm before long and as I got out the Ole Feller reminded me don't forget that coon in the back. That woke me-I suddenly remembered another "bad part" to coon hunting. I had to skin the coon and stretch the hides. We sold the pelts to buy dog . food, carbide, shells, etc. I had a few "customers" who loved to eat coon so I always saved the meat too.

I headed for the barn where I had a couple of nails and leather thongs for "game cleaning."

I don't know many, coon hunts I went on as a kid growing up in Caldwell County, Kentucky-probably over 100. The Ole Feller, Dick Long, was one of the most renowned coon hunters in that part of the country and for some reason let me become his permanent "hunting partner."

In addition to the tasks already described, this elevated position also allowed me to (1) feed his coon hounds when he was on a trip or sick, (2) clean out the dog pens, (3) walk 8 or 10 miles to the nearest farm for help whenever the pick-up got stuck, (4) build huge bond fires to dry out his clothes when he would fall through the ice, and (5) spend entire days going through the countryside looking for lost hounds which had run off chasing a deer the night before. Now that I remember back to those good ole days·it was a helluva deal.

One of the best remembered fringe benefits was that all the monthly issues of the National Cooner were passed on to me after the Ole Feller had read them and Royal Goodcare, his grown up hunting partner, had read them. I'll never forget an article I read in one issue. I decided to put that article to work and it "backfired." The article described how this feller up in Illinois used roman candles to scare coon out of his corn fields. I reasoned, if roman candles could scare a coon out of a corn field-well ...why not scare one out of a tree?

It was mid December and there was a "fireworks stand" in town where I attended school and I. bought a 20 shot roman candle to take on the next coon hunt, That night the Ole Feller came by and picked me up and we headed for the woods. Royal Goodcare had to work so there was just the two of us. I laid the roman candle in the back of the truck and didn't mention It or my plans for its uses. Since it was dark, I was able to conceal it from the Ole Feller all night-until I lit it.

We had already "kotched" two coons as the Ole Feller would say-one of them was in 'a small sapling which I was able to climb without difficulty and the other one elected to fight it out on the ground. It was getting late and the hounds were out in the middle of Clear Creek bottoms barking the familiar chop, chopping short bark which meant "coon up a tree." As we approached the hounds, I knew we had problems because we were in the tall timber of that bottom land woods. Sure enough, we shined the light up the giant sycamore tree and there was the coon's eyes-about 60 feet up.

I backed away from the tree almost twenty feet and pulled the roman candie out of my hip boot where I had been carrying it and struck the fuse to the flame of the carbide lamp. When the fire started spewing I whirled the candle a time or two and pointed it toward the coon. KAPOOF! KAPOOF! . KAPOOF! Twenty times the roman candle made the muffled explosion sound and sent the fireballs toward the heavens. While I was firing fireballs at the coon, as the Ole Feller would say, "all hell was cuttin' loose around that sycamore tree."

There had been two coons in the tree, we just didn't see the second one-the cowardly one. It only took one or two balls of fire shooting up at him and he decided to haul ring tail down the tree trunk-right into a pack of hounds. During the commotion of this coon fight, the other coon jumped out of the tree and almost lit on the Ole Feller (around shot 12 or 13 I would say). One of the hounds ran over Ole Feller In his zeal to catch coon number two.

The Ole Feller was right in the middle of the coons and hound dogs waging war with one another and he was yelling some unkind things at me in addition to ordering me to get the dogs off him. At shot 20 as my "cannon" finally fizzled out, I waded into the fight and retrieved the Ole Feller. After he got to his feet and wheezed for breath a minute or so he was able to find his - flask of liquid tranquilizer and take a long swallow of the amber substance. He was about to settle down to normal -. when he sniffed the air and said, "I smell smoke!"

We looked out in the woods in the direction I had been firing and there were about a dozen miniature "forest fires"-already lit and about to get going good. I took off my coat and ran to the nearest fire and beat it out while the Ole Feller was stomping out one of the smaller fires with his hip boots.

After about ten frantic minutes all the fires were put out and the Ole Feller needed another shot from the flask. This time, however, the effects were different-he gave me a mean look and said, "Catch the hounds and tie the lead chains to' them; We're goin to the, house."

After we were comfortably "settled in the old pickup truck and headed home the Ole Feller started chuckling and then broke out. in a laugh. "Boy,"- he said, "where do you come up with all your wild ideas?" I replied, "there was this story in last month's National Cooner ... "Never mind," the Ole Feller interrupted, "now I understand the plot hound idea you had last Fall too." But that is another story ...

CHAPTER 12

"ALMOST" LOST IN THE WOODS

After I had been coon hunting a few times with the Old Feller, I naturally had to explain to my classmates (probably eighth graders) what an expert I had become in "kotching" those ring tailed bandits. Several of the boys in my Class wanted to go along on a real coon hunt with the Old Feller and me. I promised them a hunt. However, when I told the Old Feller about it-he exploded! "Boy," he said, "don't you know I don't take strangers hunting with me! They hoot and holler and ruin the young coon hounds, and besides," he continued, "they find out the good huntin places and tell other coon hunters and before you know it-the woods will be overrun with all the coon hunters all the way from Evansville (Indiana) to Nashville (Tennessee)."

When I explained to my classmates that the Old Feller was sort of a loner and didn't take crowds on coon hunts, they were very disappointed. We talked awhile and it was suggested a time or two that maybe I had not ever been coon hunting with the Old Feller myself-matter of fact, they even began to question my knowledge of coon huntin! That was too much for my pride so I blurted out "Everybody meet at our farm at 7:00 p.m. tonight and we'll go on the biggest coon hunt you ever heard of." That got them excited again and we started planning the hunt. I instructed them on what to wear and bring-long johns, heavy coats, hip boots-and bring lights (car-bide lamps preferred) and somebody bring a .22 rifle. "What about dogs?" Asked Rod Lamb. (I planned to "borrow" three or four of the Old Feller's blue-tick hounds but remembering his tirade when I "invited" the boys on a hunt I knew I had better not "borrow" any of his. dogs.) So I said without thinking it through - "Everyone bring a dog-if you ain't got one-just catch a stray dog and bring him." I followed up by assuring them that dogs were like people-they would "follow the leader" and all be treeing coons before the night was over.

Well sir, the boys and dogs started showing up in the front yard of our farm house at about 6:30 p.m. It was already very cold-about 10° below zero and as each one showed up they tied their dog to a post on the front porch and came in by the fire to get warm. By 7:00 p.m. we had six coon hunters gathered round the wood fire and seven "coon dogs" barking and howling on the front porch and my mother about to have a "conniption" in the kitchen. My dad went outside to "hush up" the dogs and came back in the house in defeat. He strongly advised us to "commence our hunt" and get that pack of dogs out of earshot in a hurry. He also muttered a few choice words about our "coon hounds" as we filed out into the cold.

I lit the lantern and began to understand dad's muttering. There in the light was a collie, a german shepherd, a bulldog, and four "Heinz 57" variety cur dogs. We walked past our barn and I stopped and unfastened Lance (short for Sir Lancelot), dad's liver spotted pointer bird dog. There was more barking and straining at leashes (ropes) as - Lance walked around stiff legged and checked out the other dogs. We almost had a dog fight when he tried to smell the German shepherd but that was averted by a yank on the "tow rope" as we again started out.

We kept the dogs "in tow" as we moved south towards Caney Creek. I had explained beforehand that we would start hunting along Caney Creek and go east along the creek for a couple of miles then turn south again and hunt across Pea Ridge and then drop down in the Piney Creek bottoms and hunt back west and then cut north to the house. This was some pretty rugged country but I had squirrel hunted it many times and figured we could make this circle in about four to four and a half hours.

Despite our walking at a steady pace and constant struggle to keep the dogs from getting tangled and lighting, we were cold. Our breath came out in big clouds of steam and it felt like the, temperature was continuing to drop. Some of the boys were not all that well dressed for the cold either. Two of them didn't wear caps and their ears were starting to get frost bit and three of them didn't wear gloves. They could at least put their hands in their pockets-ears are another matter though.

When we stopped and unleashed the hounds their reaction was not at all like I expected. The Old Feller's coon hounds always went off a ways, had a B.M., scratched around a minute and ran off into the woods and started hunting for coons. These dogs tonight didn't act that way at all; the collie just stood there, one of the cur dogs wanted to play, the German shepherd headed back the way we came, and Lance and the other three cur dogs went out into the woods a ways and stood there. The bull dog just sat down in disgust. Next thing I knew I smelled smoke-Jim Bell couldn't stand his cold ears any longer and had started a fire. Most of the other boys started throwing leaves and dead limbs on it and before long we had a roaring camp fire going-felt good too-at least on one side. Your back side would roast while your front side froze. It wasn't long before all the dogs had gathered around the fire with us (except the German shepherd who was smart enough to go back home.)

While we stood around the fire we discussed our strategy (or was it tactics?). A.J. Sizemore had a scarf which he donated to the "cap less" boys. They cut it into strips and wrapped it around their ears. I explained to them that the dogs, being untrained in coon hunting, were not going to hunt so long as we stayed in one spot (around a fire at that). They reluctantly agreed to put . out the fire and move on. We started down the creek bank in single file, boy, dog, boy, dog, etc. I would stop ever now and then and pick up a rock and fling it out in the woods and tell Lance-"Sic em." After a couple of exploratory trips out into the woods, Lance lost interest and was content to stay at my side or visit with the collie-a lady dog. However, the bull dog was giving him lots of competition for her favors.

We had made it down Caney Creek and crossed over Messimore bridge and were moving along Pea Ridge when Rodney Lamb yelled-"Stop! Listen." A couple of hundred yards off to our left one of the cur dogs was barking. Suddenly it wasn't so cold as we moved downhill toward the barking dog. One of the boys had a five cell flashlight and he spotted the dog's eyes a long way through the woods-when we got to the dog seven lights were pointed skyward in the persimmon tree and all soon were riveted to the lone occupant of the tree-a possum. Bang! Before we knew what happened Buddy Hazel had fired the .22 rifle and the possum hit the ground with a dull thud. Buddy picked it up by its rat like tail and hoisted him high for all to admire. That's one memorable sight-a dead possum in the light of six carbide lamps and a five cell flashlight. (Probably one that few of you dear readers ever saw or ever will see.) We admired the possum for a few minutes and petted the cur dog that treed it before moving back up the hill. Of course everyone perked up at our great success and we all started bragging and talking big. "Ringtails, you better find your dens fast-the coon hunters are comin to get your hides."

We continued to walk and talk for what seemed like hours. Too late, I realized that we weren't really going anywhere-we were just walking. I shined my light in every direction-nothing was familiar. A cloud had blacked out the half moon and it was mighty dark in those woods. A hoot owl hooted off in the distance and I began to feel very, very lost. Buddy Boyd sensed something wasn't just right and asked. "Are we lost Bill?"

"Naw," I said, "just temporarily turned around a bit" I confidently headed off in the woods in what I thought was a westerly direction. We walked about an hour again before stopping for a breather. I assured everybody that the ·farm was just over the next hill (we had been going over several hills the past hour.) While we were milling around Buddie Boyd said, "We're sure enough lost-this is the spot where we were an hour ago-there's that big birch tree where I emptied my carbide lamp and there is the pile of spent carbide."

With that final bit of evidence I admitted that we were now a whole lot "turned around" and everybody got scared, tired, hungry and awfully cold. While we were trying to decide our next • move, I remembered what the Old Feller had taught me about getting nighttime lost-build a big fire, stay comfortable, and wait for' daylight. I told the boys this and before long we had a roaring fire going and were huddled around it. As we began to thaw out one by one, Carrol Taylor (who was on the "heavy" side) said, "I'm so hungry I could eat one of them dogs." Buddy Hazel threw the dead possum over to Carroll and said, "Eat this possum if you are so hungry-I hear they are good eatin."

Carrol got out his pocket knife and started to dress the possum. Naturally, he didn't know how so I ended up doing most of the "dressing." There was a ditch nearby and we found a hole large enough that Carrol could break the ice (with his superior weight) and we jiggled the possum carcass in the water a few times to clean it. Carroll had whittled out a skewer stick and soon had the possum cooking over the camp fire. It sizzled and popped and every time a drop of grease fell into the fire it immediately flared up and cast a glow over Carroll's hungry face. Carroll finally took the meat off the fire and cut a piece off with his pocket knife-and ate it. He pronounced it well done and ready and started passing chunks around to the rest of us as the poor, tired, cold and hungry dogs looked on. It was tough and greasy but I think (not sure) that everyone of us choked-down a few bites before we started to sneak the pieces that Carroll continued to gleefully whack off the carcass and pass around to us to the hungry dogs. Finally, there was no more meat-just bones.

In a few minutes, Doug Hamby, who always did have a weak stomach, left the campfire and got a few feet into the woods before he "lost his supper." When the odor of this made it back to the fire it was all any of us could do to hold ours down. We tried telling jokes, etc. to keep our minds occupied and A.J. Sizemore remembered reading once in a book about how trappers in the north country would be down with their sled dogs when they spent the night out on their trap lines. The heat of the dogs bodies kept them warm, so AJ. said. That was the best idea of the night, we thought-so we got up and started raking up a huge pile of leaves about ten feet from the fire. We threw a . few more dead limbs on the, fire and started catching dogs. One by one each of us burrowed into that pile of leaves dragging a dog in behind us. After much thrashing about things finally settled down and, though not comfortable, it was tolerable inside that pile of leaves. We actually did get some sleep-all except Doug who finally crawled out and spent the night keeping the fire going. At the crack of day he was kicking in' the pile of leaves-getting us up. Doug couldn't understand how we could sleep while he stood by the fire the past hour firing the .22 rifle and yelling at the top of his lungs. We asked "why?" He said he had heard gunshots off in the distance about an hour ago and they were getting closer. While he was talking, my dad, Uncle Calvin, and Tom Boyd came walking into our "camp".

At first, Dad gave me a scolding for (1) getting lost and (2) taking his pet birddog, Lance, out "coon hunting." However, as we started describing our experiences of the night before, the adults began to see the humor of it all, despite the fact they had been out looking for us since midnight. We were truly lost, about three miles from Piney Creek off on the Hunsaker place.

As we were making the long walk back home, I couldn't help thinking, that possum wouldn't taste too bad if you had some salt, pepper, and mom's hot sauce to go on it.....

CHAPTER 13

THE MOST VALUABLE COON HOUND IN TEXAS

Cecil Coter and Rivets Redden grew up on adjoining farms southeast of Tenaha, Panola County, Texas. Even though they were the best of friends, they always fought and argued--right on through manhood. Both became farmers and lived near one another. Probably the most common thing between them was their love for coon hunting. It was fitting that each of them, at one time or another, would own the most valuable coon hound that ever lived in Texas. The story goes like this.

Rivets had taken a load of chickens to Centre to sell, and he got a right good price for them. After he bought some whiskey and kicked up his heels some, he decided to head back home. He loaded his Ford stake bed truck and pulled out of Centre about dark. He wasn't drunk, but he wasn't exactly sober either; and, since it was dusk, it wouldn't have been too safe to try to cross the road ahead of him. Anyway, he made it to Tenaha and was on the dirt road to home when Cecil tried to do just that--he was going across the road from the pasture to the barnyard and his coon hound was walking alongside. Rivets saw them, but too late-he hit the brakes and started a skiddin' and a sliding. Cecil saw what was about to happen, and he jumped. Rivets missed him, but really made glue factory ammunition out of the old coon hound and battered in the front end of the old Ford.

Rivets got out of the truck to survey the damage; and in a few minutes Cecil recovered from his shock and started cussin and a threatening rivets with a lawsuit, bodily harm, and other things too terrible to mention.

Rivets was feeling no pain, so he didn't pay too much attention to Cecil's threats. However, he did catch some things that Cecil said and that was that the old coon hound had a little pup and that he was a murderer and a thief and was leaving this little critter motherless to die. Wal, old Rivets really had a soft spot for animals; and this story really touched him. He asked Cecil where the pup was; and, when told that he was at the barn, he wanted to see him. Cecil said, "OK, but we'll walk. If you drive that truck over there, I'm afraid you'll knock the whole damn barn down." They went over to the barn and saw the little black and tan critter laying in some straw. Rivets said, "How much will you take for this little scrub pup?"

Cecil said, "You mean how much will I settle for that fine registered black and tan hound lying out there deader than a doornail and this future field trail champion? Why, you dumb chicken rancher, you ain't got enough money to even buy their collars!"

Rivets said, "Hell, Cecil, I don't want their equipment or that fancy buildup--all I want is this scrawny, little pup that are goin' to die anyhow; and the only reason I want him is 'cause I' feel kind of guilty; and, I want to bottle feed him and see if I can save him." Cecil said, "You are crazy as hell on top of being dumb. Do you think I'm going to stand by for your running over the best hound dog that ever walked the earth and then give you her pup? I would have sold that mother and pup for $1,000 cold cash!

Rivets remembered that he still had a little over $300 of his "chicken money" that he was taking home to the old lady and said, "I'll give you $200 for the both of em, and you can have the mother back if you'll haul her off for me." "Sold" said Cecil before Rivets could change his mind, "Where's my money?" Sam pulled out his "chicken money" and peeled off ten $20 bills. He took the pup in the cab of the truck with him and proceeded on to his farm down the road.

Well sir, when Rivets got home with that unweaned, orphan puppy, there was such a commotion and fuss made over him by the kids and the wife that it was days before Mrs. Redden realized that all the "chicken money" had been spent on that scrawny puppy which was by now a full-fledged member of the family. Everyone in the family took turns feeding the pup, which by now had been called, Blackie, Midnight but finally and lastly, "Bugler, which name stuck.

Soon after the accident and transaction, Cecil Coter sold his farm and took a job in Houston. Ten years passed and Bugler grew into a fine deep mouthed coon hound which gave Rivets hours of pleasure hearing him chase the ring tail bandits of the night.

In the meantime, things had changed around Centre. The state had bought some land around there and built a nice lake and park, and a few tourists had begun to visit during the summer. Some had evidently liked it there, because they just upped and moved there to live (mostly, retired folks on government pensions).

One of them that moved in up the road from the Reddens was Cecil Coter. He and Rivets got to renew their friendship since Cecil liked to sample bourbon once in a while, and he would come over to Rivets house and sample his. Rivets didn't mind, cause he liked to hear Cecil tell about all the exciting things that had happened to him in the years he spent in Houston.

One night when Cecil came over and they were having a snort or two; and Cecil was telling of the time he got into a bar room brawl in a dive by the ship channel, Rivets made a big mistake. He tried to borrow some money from Cecil. Cecil changed the subject back to Houston very rapidly, but Rivets persisted. Cecil was finally forced to face reality and asked, "How much you need, Rivets?" Rivets said he had to have $300 to pay the dentist for what he owed him for some store-bought teeth, or he feared that the dentist (who had made several attempts to collect already) would take the teeth away from him.

Cecil studied the situation for a minute and finally squinted his eyes and looked at Rivets and said, "Rivets, I'll tell you what I'm going to do- I'm going to pay you $300 for that old coon hound that you have." Rivets said, "Oh no I could never sell Bugler." There was silence for several minutes, and it. suddenly dawned on Rivets that Cecil wasn't going to loan him a dime much less $300. Reality can be a brutal thing, and reality hit Rivets right in the pocketbook about then. He finally said, "Cecil, if you promise to take good care of Bugler and not sell him, I'll let you have him for $500." (Cecil had long forgotten about the transaction 10 years past and did not realize who Bugler was). Cecil said, "$100." Rivets said, "$450." Cecil, "$150:" Rivets, "$400." Cecil, "$250." Rivets, "$300, and not a damn cent cheaper." Cecil, "$300." Rivets, "Sold!"

Who knows what possessed Cecil to buy the old dog. Maybe it was because he was still so friendly and maybe his subconscious mind was telling him who Bugler was. Maybe Cecil wanted to help his old friend, Rivets; but he was afraid that a $300 loan would turn into a "bad debt": and if he bought the dog he would have something tangible in place of his departed tangible money. Like I say-who knows why? At any rate, the contract was made; Cecil led old Bugler off that night; and Rivets had his "store-bought teeth" money in pocket.

Rivets didn't sleep much that night, all he could think about was his dear, departed friend, Bugler. Early the next morning he was knocking on Cecil's door. He wanted to swap back-teeth or no teeth. Cecil said, "No-a trade was a trade." They got into a bitter argument and it ended when Cecil said he wouldn't sell Bugler under any condition--except maybe for $800. Rivets left, determined to hustle up another $500 some way or another and get old Bugler back.

Rivets spent the next several days figuring how he could come up with another $500, and Cecil spent the next few days getting better acquainted and quite attached to Bugler. Finally, Rivets hit upon an idea. The old lady had accumulated several quilts which she had sewn over the years, and he decided that he would sneak them out of the closet and sell them to the tourists. He had seen a few peddlers at the park entrance from time to time selling chalk statues, felt pictures, and chenille bedspreads; and he figured if the tourists suckers would buy that stuff-surely they would buy some genuine handmade quilts!

His plans were made on this basis; and he made some signs, "Genuine handmade quilts--$100 a piece." When the old lady went to gather the eggs Saturday morning, he "stole" five quilts from the closet and put them in the cab of his pickup truck. After a while he used the excuse that he had to go to town to pay the dentist and take a saw to the shop to get it sharpened; and left with the merchandise. He drove to the park entrance and set up shop the way he had seen the peddlers do it. He stretched a rope between two trees and hung the quilts on it. He then placed his signs leaning up against the trees and the pickup. He filled his pipe, lit it, and sat down on the running board of the pickup to enjoy the pipe and wait for customers.

Business was sort of slow since the "tourist season" was not in full swing, nevertheless he sold 3 quilts that day. Sunday, with the excuse that he was going fishing (supported by two cane poles tied on the side of his truck), he again went down to the park entrance and set up shop. His luck changed, for by noon he had sold both quilts and had an order for another one. He returned to the farm in the highest of spirits (which the missus found hard to understand since he had no fish and said they weren't biting). After he ate, he went directly to his neighbor. Cecil, and presented the $800. Cecil wouldn't take the money at first; but when he saw the toothless grin on Rivets face turn into a very threatening scowl, he decided that "a trade was a trade"--and he took the money. Rivets triumphantly led old Bugler home.

A few weeks passed, and the experience of the dog trade had kind of put a damper on the friendship between Rivets and Cecil. Cecil (who was a widower) began to get lonesome and longed for Rivets companionship and for the friendly licks of old Bugler. He could stand it no longer and went over to Rivets with the excuse (really a sincere one) that he wanted to buy old Bugler back.

Rivets mellowed somewhat upon seeing the sincerity in Cecil and finally agreed to sell Bugler to him so that he would have a companion. However, the conditions were that Rivets could come over and see him anytime he wished--and the purchase price was raised to $1,000. Cecil didn't have that kind of cash-but he had a blank check; and he carefully wrote out a check on the Commercial Bank of Tenaha payable to Rivets for $1,000. This was on a Saturday, and the bank was closed, but Rivets took the check on the basis of a rumor which he had heard from the local barber, Slim Atcheson, who said that he had heard that Cecil had at least $10,000 in the bank.

Cecil led old Bugler off again. The next morning Rivets decided that he would go over and check on Cecil and Bugler. Cecil wasn't friendly at all and refused to let Rivets go out to the shed and see the old dog. (That night the thought of paying $1,000 for a dog was too much for Cecil).

Rivets said, "All right, you lousy welsher! If I can't see your dog, then I'll just buy him back. What will you take for him?" Cecil did some quick arithmetic and decided if Rivets raised the price on him, turn about was fair play--he said, "$5,000."

Rivets didn't bat an eye. He gave Cecil his $1,000 check back and then pulled out a bland check on the Commercial Bank of Tenaha and commenced to write out a check to Cecil for $4,000. Cecil commenced to get a little uneasy, for he didn't think Rivets could cash a check for $400 at the bank--much less $4,000.

When Rivets handed the check to Cecil, Cecil really got uneasy and said, "Is this check any good? Rivets-got red in the face and said, "You welcher--I took your check, didn't I?" Cecil said, "OK, Rivets--don't get hot" and took the check. However, the wheels were already. starting to turn.

Later on that afternoon he was knocking on Rivets door' and when Rivets invited him in and served him a little bourbon and brandy, the subject of old Bugler entered the conversation. Finally, Cecil said, "Rivets, I've just got to have that dog back, and I'll give you $10,000 for him." Rivets thought it over for a minute and finally said, "OK, neighbor, he's yours if you promise to let me come see him' everyday and, also, you agree to sell him back to me if I have to have him back."

They shook hands, and Cecil returned Rivets $4,000 check and wrote him another for $6,000. It wasn't but a few days later that Rivets decided that he would buy the old dog back and keep him for good.

He went to see Cecil and the trade was made-tor $20,000. Rivets gave Cecil his $6,000 check and wrote one for $14,000.

That night old Bugler died. Rivets was grief stricken. One of the first things that he knew he must do was to tell Cecil--so off he went to perform this unpleasant duty. When he told Cecil, Cecil came unglued. He cried; he moaned; he cursed; and finally sat down and placed his elbows on his knees, his hands over his face, and cried.

Rivets stood over him and tears ran down his own cheeks, It was a very touching moment. Cecil finally looked up and said, "You know; Rivets, if old Bugler hadn't died, me and you both would have been rich men by next spring plowin' time."

D. VARMIT HUNTING

Varmits are useless little critters that are not normal game animals. They include foxes, bobcats, civet cats, coyotes, etc. There is no open season on them and most hunters never bothered to hunt them per se- although many were shot by hunters who saw them accidentally while hunting other game.

This changed along about the 50's or 60's when a couple of good ole boys in Marble Falls (the Burnham Brothers) started making and selling "Varmit calls." These calls were similar to a duck call but reproduced the cry of the wounded rabbit (when properly blown). The most popular varmit hunted is old Wily coyote.

I was introduced to the sport by a fellow deer hunter on a deer lease we had near Llano one year. I drove through Marble Falls one weekend, found the Burnams place, bought a couple of calls, and got a brief lesson in varmit calling. I have since had many unusual expenditures while varmit hunting.

CHAPTER 14

MISADVENTURES OF A VARMIT HUNTER

SHOOT KEVIN........SHOOT!

"Hush -- be very quiet," whispered to my hunting companion. "I think hear something coming In the woods," We were on our deer lease near the town of Jewell In Leon County on one of those mild November nights and I had been calling on my newly acquired Burman Bros. varmint call for probably 20 or 30 minutes. It was pitch dark and we were in a small patch of woods on a creek bank.

After a couple of minutes of silence I blew softly on the call a couple of times and there was no mistaking the noise this time. There was all sorts of leaves rustling and thrashing about In the woods - and It was getting very close. Bud Koble, my hunting partner, had the .22 rifle and light and he said -- "I'm going to turn on the light .. get ready." He did and what we saw really broke us up. We were surrounded by a herd of Brahma cattle! This was my Initiation to the art of varmint calling In the late fifties. My varmint calling techniques have improved somewhat since this initial hunt -- but In the process there have been other climaxes almost as hilarious as this first experience. Not one to brag -- I hasten to add that over the years I've skinned out a few coyote, civet cat, coon, and bobcat pelts from some of the more tone deaf critters who have been lured In by my "night music."

When I was a boy hunting squirrels, coons, foxes, etc. back in the hills of Kentucky I had the good fortune of hunting some with Uncle Josh White - a distant relative who lived alone out in the Caney Creek bottom In Caldwell County. Uncle Josh farmed a little but mostly he hunted, trapped, and fished.

I learned from him that you could produce a noise that resembled a squirrels bark by kissing the back of your hand. Sometimes, when the woods were still and quiet you could make the "noise" and have several squirrels "barking" in response to the call. He also taught me how to produce a quail "assembly whistle" noise with my lips that would call up quail -- particularly If you had flushed a covey and they were trying to regroup. And how to call crows into shooting range by imitating the hoot of an owl.

After I grew up and came to Texas I started deer and turkey hunting and had forgotten those boyhood experiences until I happened upon a varmint calling demonstration by the Burman Bros. - I think at the old Cullem & Boren store in downtown Dallas. Anyway, It fascinated me and I purchased a couple of their varmint calls and 45 rpm record of instructions and set about learning to call up varmints (and various other critters).

My learning experience with this new gadget almost broke up a relatively happy marriage and drove my bird dog to insanity. It also caused a lot of neighborhood gossip. The only record player we had was a large 33 rpm console which was In the living room. It had a 45 rpm adapter and I would place my "training" record on it and pick up the varmint call and start practicing. I would try to keep the volume very low but it just didn't work .- you had to blow full blast or nothing.

When I would start my soulful song of the dying rabbit - my bride of 3 or 4 years at that time would start yelling -- stop that racket, you woke up the babies (we had two at the time), a neighbor would be ringing the doorbell to find out who was hurt, and Pete, my bird dog, would chime in with his mournful howl out back. The result of my first field test which I described In the first paragraph 'are therefore understandable - heck fire, I never got adequate practice beforehand.

After deer season that year I starting driving out to the East Fork of the Trinity River, near Forney, and practiced on the "wolves" that were plentiful In those days. After much practice and experimenting I finally got to the point that I could actually call them in-at least some of the times I tried. However, I never took anyone else with me until I gained proficiency in the "art" of varmint calling.

As the years passed and my two sons got old enough to go deer hunting with us, became active with the Boy Scouts, etc., they and their friends became participants in some of these memorable varmint calling experiences.

One night on a Boy Scout camp out I took a group of boys out away from camp to put on a varmint calling demonstration. I had stressed silence - they all promised to be very quiet while I tried to call up a varmit. Again It was dark after calling a few times I got a response -- I called softly a couple of more times before turning on the light. When I did, one of the boys blasted out "Gee whiz, look how big that German Shepherd is!" With that, the coyote lit a shuck, of course.

One of my hunting partners on the deer lease brought his youngest son down one weekend -- he couldn't have been over 7 or 8. Alter supper we were sitting around the camp fire and got to talking about varmit calling and Kevin, the boy, became keenly interested. He insisted on going varmit hunting right now and he also Insisted on being the one who got to shoot the varmint. We had been hunting first. I got my varmint call and my hunting partner got a light and a .22 rifle and we started out. I tried calling a short way from camp but had no success. We moved further away and tried again - again no answer. About the third lime we moved, little Kevin was tired and his dad carried him to our next stop. We had agreed that If

nothing responded we were going back to camp and go to bed. We settled down on a protected side of a hill (It was a cold frosty night), Kevin with the gun, Sam with the light, and me with the varmint call and I started calling.

After several periods of alternately calling and then listening we finally got some action. Sam shined the light across the hillside and spotted eyes - cat eyes. I continued to call softer and softer as the cat circled and got closer. The next time Sam turned on the light the bobcat was no more than 15 paces away -- standing broadside with his back bowed. After what seemed minutes I whispered - "Shoot Kevin - shoot." The cat started bounding away. Sam next turned the light on Kevin and there he lay -sound asleep.

I was working at Lone Star in east Texas and went to lunch with some of the clients employees. We started discussing hunting and finally narrowed it down to varmit hunting. When I told them of some of my varmit hunting experiences they all to 60 varmit hunting with me. I always carried my hunting and fishing gear with me in these days. We agreed to go hunting Friday night. They said they would pick me up at the motel around 7 and we would drive to the river bottoms.

When they picked me up I amazed at some of the "costumes" and equipment. One of them had a camouflaged suit and carried a bow and arrow, another was wearing slacks and loafers and carrying a double barrel shotgun and the other looked like a Hollywood cowboy 10 gallon hat, cowboy boots, and carrying a .357 magnum, pearl-handled pistol In a quick-draw holster. They had one two cell flashlight between them. I knew right away that this night was going to be an experience.

On the drive over to the river bottoms I told them all of the wild stories I could think of about how people calling varmints had actually been run over or attacked by the varmints which sometimes came charging right in to the call at full gallop. I recounted my own experiences of having had my feet knocked from under me one night by a coyote who ran into me at full throttle (true), a friend who almost had a eye clawed out by a mountain lion (not true), etc. Anyway, by the time we parked the car and headed through the bottoms for the creek -- they were primed for what was to follow. We selected a spot to start calling which really was kind of spooky looking. The sound of the varmint call added to the feeling created by the surroundings. Sure enough, after a few calls we heard noise in the wood. They all started whispering back and forth despite my warnings to keep quiet. As I put the call to my lips to "coax the varmit closer" I slowly reached up above my head and got a hold on a tree limb directly over them. I blew the call a couple of more times then let out a squall as I pulled the tree lumb down on top of them and jiggled it a couple of times.

I don't know what all happened next - they left In three directions - the cowboy was blasting away with the .357 about every tenth step, Robin Hood broke his bow string, and the other feller ran out of his loafers and left them somewhere In the woods. When I got back to the car they already had the engine running. I got in and we left out In a hurry -- three of them with their legs crossed to conceal the off colored streaks down their britches legs.

Yep, varmit hunting can be mighty interesting - and downright sporting.

E. FISHING TALES

My earliest memories of fishing were of fishing with my granddad in Clifty Creek. We fished with came poles and worms for "perch." To this day I have never met anyone who loved to eat fish more than my granddad did.

My friend, Rod, and I spent one summer living in a cave on Piney Creek. (I wrote a book about this "A Summer On Piney Creek). We earned enough by catching and selling fish to buy all of our provision that summer. That was my introduction to "commercial" fishing as well as bass fishing. I made my first bass Rod out of a piece of hickory which I carved.

When I started bass fishing there weren't many of us. bass fishing in Texas exploded with the creation of the manmade lakes in the 50's and 60's along with the development of the Skeeter boats and on Toledo Bend. (The World's greatest bass hole).

Those were the good old days - particularly for fishing.

CHAPTER 15

SPRING RITUALS ON TOLEDO BEND

Every time I dump the contents of my six or seven tackle boxes on the floor to reorganize my fishing lures there are certain lures in. The heap that bring back fond memories of the many trips a group of us took to Toledo Bend. There is a wad of green jigs, a $50 Big "0", a red Little N, some homemade plastic crayfish, and many others. All of you who have fished with guides know what I'm referring to. On certain days there is only one lure that the bass will hit. and the bait shop by the dock just happened to get a fresh supply in yesterday, so at the guide's suggestion you buy ten or twelve of them before you head out. And. if you are a pack rat like me, you hang on to those you didn't hang up - forever.

I'm a C.P.A. by profession and have always been tied to my desk from mid January until April 15th each year. Back in the late 5O's a group of us who worked together planned a fishing trip during a coffee break one "busy season". We decided that right after April 15th we would go to Toledo Bend for four days of bass fishing and R and R. Being accountants, we planned the trip in detail. The planning and talking seemed to make the "busy season" pass soon - kind of like dangling a carrot in front of a rabbit.

"WE PLANNED A FISHING TRIP DURING COFFEE BREAKS ONE BUSY SEASON"

Finally the appointed time arrived and we loaded two cars and headed for the fishing camp. There were eight of us plus gear, refreshments, groceries, and all the other usual "things" for such a trip. Thus began a spring ritual that continued for the next fifteen years or so. There probably was not an experienced "big water" fisherman in the group. I don't think any of us had fished with a guide before and a couple of boys had never been fishing -period. You can imagine what the subject at the morning coffee drinking and bull session of the local guides was for the next couple of weeks - "that bunch of amateurs out of Dallas".

Certain rituals and precedents were set that first trip that continued for the next fifteen years and included -

(1). An all night poker game the first night in camp

(2). We always took too many groceries and not enough beverages

(3). Fishing contests with "flexible" rules

(4). At least one day of stormy weather (out of the three or four days we normally stayed).

(5). At -least one case of bad sunburn (or windburn), one case of "sea sickness", and at least one lure hooked in someone's ear, hand, etc.

One of the cabins we rented had a kitchen and that cabin became our "headquarters". We did all our cooking, eating, card playing, storytelling, etc. in it and slept in other cabins. When we checked in they told us to meet our guides at the dock at 6:00 a.m, so we decided that it would be necessary to arise at 4:00 AM in order to prepare and consume a hearty breakfast, get our fishing gear together, and be at the dock on time. We knew not to be late - the guides might leave without us. We all pitched in and unpacked and got the kitchen squared away so that the cook (me) could never find whatever he needed to prepare the meal. Some of the ingredients would always vanish (such as graham crackers needed for the banana pudding) so that constant trips to the store also became part o the ritual.

Unpacking completed, we then had an "organization" meeting to decide on the fishing contest rules, who was going to fish together - and with which guides. The contest finally came down to two pots - one for the largest fish and one for the most fish. Since there were eight of us and four guides, it started getting complicated - especially since they also told us when we checked in that the four guides we had scheduled for Saturday and Sunday would not be with us on Monday and Tuesday - they were locating some more guides to fill in those days. Finally one of the more innovative C.P.A.'s in our group got a pencil and piece of paper and worked out a schedule whereby we not only changed fishing guide each half day - we also changed fishing partners, Kind of like musical bass boats, it took some time to get all that figured out and we also put a dent in the beverage supply in the process. However, after we got everything "organized", we cleared the table and started a serious poker game.

Again, someone had brought some plastic chips and another schedule was set up for keeping track of your pluses and minuses as a result of your participation in the poker playing. The game started rather civilized - five card stud or draw with an occasional hand of seven card stud .if someone got up to bleed their lizard or something. After an hour or so it always reverted to uncivilized games such as Red Dog, Booray, Anaconda and Hi/Lo Split. We were having so much fun that time got away from us - someone suddenly spoke up and said- "My goodness-it's 4:30A.M. already, we better quit and fix breakfast". Of course some of the losers continued to play while the winners volunteered to cook. We finally served the bacon, eggs, biscuits, and coffee and the game broke up. We finished breakfast, stacked the dishes in the sink, grabbed our fishing gear and headed to the boat dock. Since we didn't stop at the camp restaurant, the guides hadn't seen us, so naturally they weren't waiting at the dock. We waited till a quarter past six and finally one of the group walked up the hill to the camp office (store and restaurant in same building) to find out what the problem was. He met the guides and they came down the hill together. They eyeballed us pretty good and we finally got all paired up.

The guides that Jerry and I drew wanted to examine our fishing gear and lures. He flat refused to let me bring my Zebco aboard his boat and ordered us to go back to the store and get some green jigs with white skirts and a bag of ice. We trotted up the hill and obeyed his orders and I also purchased a bait casting rod and reel and some line while there. We went back to the dock and he was sitting there in his boat with the engine running - looking put out and impatient. The rest of our group had the same experience but two of the boats had already gotten away from the dock ahead of us.

I spent the next thirty minutes on a hair raising boat ride down Toledo Bend (maybe I should have used a different description) - anyway it was a fast ride and I was busily trying to wind the line on my new reel as we rode - impossible.

We finally stopped abruptly and before we realized what was happening the guide had caught a bass. My, he was fast. We didn't even know he was going to fish. He caught a nice mess of fish before I was rigged up and ready to start fishing. Jerry had a spinning rod and had also caught three or four bass while I was frantically winding line on my reel. Jerry would yell — "Get the net, get the net!" The guide would say sarcastically, "Net, hell, that fish ain't big enough to bend a Bass rod". I would interrupt my line winding to net Jerry's fish and the guide would chuckle and spit tobacco juice. Finally I had my new rod and reel ready to go and drew back for a powerful cast to a spot where the guide had just caught a nice bass. (Naturally I was in the back seat — some sixteen feet farther away from the "honey hole" than the guide. Anyway, I got what I truly believe to be the worst backlash on my very first cast that I have ever seen. I sat there dejected and tried to unravel the mess. The guide let me pick at it for at least thirty minutes. I finally threw the rod down and popped a beer and offered him one. He finally took pity and said — "Heck fire, I got an extra rod in the storage bin — use it!" He even stopped fishing, picked up my rod and cut anyway the bird nest and wrapped a new tine on it while I fished. The ice was melting and we all three were soon in a friendly conversation. He turned out to be an all right feller once you got to know him. The fish quit biting so he cranked up the outboard and we moved to another spot and fished — then another, then another — some would be a mile or so apart. Finally he said it was time to head to the dock so he started the opposite direction from the dock — so I thought. That's how turned around had gotten on that huge body of water. We were real proud of our morning "catch" (most of which had been caught by our guide). The other boats were already in and our proud catch was pitiful compared to the "catch" that one of the boats brought in. (I decided right there which guide I wanted to fish with that afternoon.) The guides told us that they took a mid-day break and we should be back at the dock at 4:00 P.M. for the afternoon trip. We didn't argue. We went back to the cabin, ate some sandwiches, argued over the schedule and finally ended up changing it after a bunch of coin flips, and then went to bed for a much needed nap.

We all hated to get up from those beds when the alarm went off at 3:45 P.M. but finally did and drug ourselves back to the docks. Next followed a bunch- of scrambling as we moved rods, reels, tackle boxes, beer, etc., from one boat to another. The guides were somewhat bewildered by our "shift" but became belligerent when we tried to move the fish. They flat objected so we decided to use the "honor" system for

- 133 -

the size and quantity of fish reported for the contest (That proved to be a mistake - all were not honorable when it came to a $16 pot).

As we pulled away from the dock this time we were (or felt we were) experienced "pros". We had stopped by the tackle shop and got some leads, hooks and plastic worms like the guides were using and bought some baseball caps which we now had turned around backwards as we "split the wind" in the race down Toledo Bend. I was fishing with Ike that afternoon and our guide was an "opposite" from the one I had in the morning. He told us exactly what to do and I expected a report card from him at the end of the day. However, since I had never done any "worm fishing" before; that afternoon I got a good indoctrination in that "art" and even caught a few fish. As usual, the big one got away. I had about a fifteen pound bass (eyeball weight - probably about six pounds on a scale) right up to the boat and he got off as we tried to land him. (I think Ike knocked him off with the net.) Ike caught a five and one half pound grinnel which he promptly proclaimed the winner of the big fish pot. We followed the same pattern of that morning - fish awhile - move to another spot - fish awhile - move to another spot. By now I was beginning to get my bearings and starling to recognize certain landmarks (and lakermarks). When we returned to the dock that night - our boat had the most fish. We were also in for a pleasant surprise - the guides cleaned the fish!! They had electric knives whirring and filleting about two bass a minute when we walked up to the fish cleaning shack. That was amazing to me - I knew it would have taken us till midnight to clean those fish. (Later I mastered the art of filleting bass with an electric knife.)

SO.. WHAT IF NOBODY KNOWS WHAT IT IS..... I STILL WIN BIG FISH !!

That night we had a steak dinner and short poker game. We were all very tired. Another precedent started too. It turned out that every one of us snored in our sleep - some worse than others of course. Each night thereafter there was an unannounced (and never discussed) race to try to get to sleep first. If three or four of the really good snorers got going good before you fell asleep - it became very difficult to do so. Matter of fact, one year someone snuck a tape recorder along on the trip and stayed up one night and made a tape of the snoring symphony along with solos of each member of the orchestra. It was a, riot when he played it back to us the next day. I think he still has the tape and know he has played it before at his Lions Club, in later years.

The first day established the pattern for the next three days. Fishing from 6:00 to about 11:00 a.m. a five hour mid day break - and then fishing from 4:00 to about 8:00 p.m.; mixed in was an early morning breakfast, a noon lunch of sandwiches, followed by a good nap a big supper followed by a couple of hours of poker and then to bed.

Each day we learned more about Toledo Bend, fishing, fishing guides, each other. and ourselves. Of all the trips we took - the first one was probably the best. We caught a lot of fish - not because of Toledo Bend. Little did we realize that we were fishing the old gal at her peak - anybody could catch a lot of fish if they half tried. The last night there we had a big fish fry - boy, did those freshly caught fish taste great. We decided to leave at noon the fourth day. The weather had turned bad and the lake was white capping - and besides, we were tired. We spent about thirty minutes haggling over the winners of the contest. Since the rules weren't clear, Ike finally prevailed on the big fish pot with his grinnel and Ken won the most fish pot because he had caught a bunch of bream off the dock one day during the noon break with some crickets he bought at the bait shop. We voted to close those "loopholes" so such underhanded tactics couldn't prevail another year. We finally got packed, including an ice chest crammed full of bass filets, and headed back to Dallas. Within a few miles everyone was asleep except the drivers. The trip home was uneventful I think - I slept all the way.

The next day was a work day and at coffee break we started planning another t rip for the following spring. And so it went for fifteen years. Of course, the original eight fishermen did not stay together on the same job for fifteen years. We each went our own way over the years and some moved to distant places. Usually when that happened, we had an ample supply of substitutions who wanted to join us. Some years we would have last minute cancellations and end with seven or even eight making the trip. Following are some of the incidents I recall from those subsequent trips.

Fishing guides that stand out include one bewhiskered gentleman who never bathed. When he was upwind of you in the boat it was tough to concentrate on fishing. We would ask him to move the boat this way or that with his trolling motor so we could get a better cast -the maneuver, of course, was to post him downwind. We really had some serious coin flips to see who had to fish with him, even though he was a good fisherman.

There was another guide who was an ex-teacher that really studied the sport - made a science of it. He taught us much and later wrote articles and books on the subject. He was highly respected by all and we were always eager to draw his boat.

And there were two or three guides who entered the tournament trail and later became famous among bass tournament fishermen. One of them I especially remember for his aggressive fishing - he always maneuvered the boat for himself and tried to catch all the fish in the lake. You were excess baggage in his bass boat. After a couple of hours of that nonsense I ordered him back to the dock and refused to ever set foot in his boat again.

And there was the lame old gentleman who rarely ever fished. He did everything in his power to help us catch fish -gave instructions that usually worked, maneuvered the boat so that we could cast to the best spots, etc. He was a good story teller and kept us entertained with stories of his past experiences.

The female guide that we used a couple of years was as good a fisher person as the men. She was tough and could cuss like a sailor. If anyone moved in on her fishing spot - particularly "Bug Island" - she would have the air blue in a second or two as she gave them instructions to move on.

In the later years, we had the misfortune of scheduling trips on weekends when there were Bass Tournaments being held on the lake. I grew to hate those tournaments with a passion. One of our guides was a retired railroad engineer and was a large robust man was felt the same.

One day we were in a quiet cove catching a few fish when a tournament boat roared into the cove at full speed and stopped about twenty feet from us and started fishing. Our guide told the two tournament fishermen what he thought of them and an argument ensued which ended when both boats went to the bank and our guides got out and proceeded to whip hell out of both of them.

All in all, guides, I finally concluded are just people. If you treated them with respect and friendship - they reciprocated in kind.

We gradually did less and less cooking and started eating out more at the camp restaurant and local eateries. We found a barbeque joint across the lake in Louisiana that made delicious barbeque - although I'm convinced it was made from wild hog and venison. It still tasted great. I suppose one of the reasons we started to eat out more was Eric's gravy. Eric was one of the substitutes I told you about and for a couple of months before one trip all he talked about in our planning session was the great cream gravy he was going to fix for our breakfast. Well when he finally did cook some of his gravy, you couldn't pour it out of the skillet or dig ,it out with a spoon. It was kind of jello like in consistency and tasted like that guide I described a few minutes ago.

About as scared as I ever got was on one trip when we decided to fish on our own without guides. The last couple of trips had not been all that great - the quality of guides seemed to diminish each year and the fishing had been terrible. By then most of us had become "pros" ourselves and several of us owned bass boats. Anyway, on this particular trip we got up the first day and the weather was bad and the prediction was for even worse weather. However, we had been cooped up all winter in an office and a little foul weather wasn't going: to stop us from fishing. We loaded into the boats and headed down the lake in rough water. We found some shore line down the lake that was "fishable" and started to fish. We had agreed before we left to stay together because of the weather.

LET ME SEE.....
THE PH FACTOR DIVIDED
BY TWO-MULTIPLIED BY
10 MPH WINDS WITH
MINOR WAVE ACTION
WITH THE MOON
ON THE DECREASE
EQUALS...

BIG BASS

DON KIRKLAND

ONE GUIDE STUDIED FISHING—AN
MADE A SCIENCE OF IT!

We caught a few fish but they had quit biting and we decided to move. When we pulled out into the main body of the lake it was like the North Atlantic - a strong wind was blowing out of the north - cold! - and the whitecaps were thick. It was starting to rain, the thunder was clapping and the lightning flashing. We signaled each other by hand and started back toward fishing camp some four miles up the lake. We were soon in Sabine Pass - an area where the lake narrows, and I'm not kidding - the waves coming through the pass were no different from those on any ocean - about five to six feet high. Bass boats were bobbing up and down like corks as we struggled to move northward. Soon my boat was almost full of water, the bilge pump turning but making very little progress, and my normally reliable Johnson outboard was coughing now and again as the gas tank floated around with Bob trying to catch it. We were both soaked and frozen, and scared stiff. My hand was literally frozen to the throttle. To this day I don't know how we made it back to the dock - but we did. We tied up and sloshed our way back to the cabin and headed straight to the showers and turned on the hot water. We got into the shower fully clothed to "thaw out." Soon we were thawed and in dry clothes. A stiff shot of Mr. J.W. Dant had us back to near normal. We ate lunch and settled down to an afternoon of poker as it continued to rain outside. To this day you can't get me out on a big lake when there is even a threat of rain. (Although I have had storms sneak up on me since.)

Here it is January again and I'm about to start another tax season. Fellow's, let's get together next Saturday and plan another trip to Toledo Bend for late April. I need a carrot to pull me through.

CHAPTER 16

CAMPING ON THE CREEK BANK

There aren't many sounds more exciting to me than those made by a few hungry bass as they slash through a school of shad or bait fish on the surface. Even the sound of a single bass catching a frog or minnow on the surface is enough to get my juices flowing. These sounds are enough to cause most fishermen to unzip the warm sleeping bag. hit the cold ground, pull on his britches, hop in the boat, and "get after em". Assuming, of course, that you are camping amongst em and within earshot of those wonderful sounds.

I have been camping out for many years and have done every kind, from backpacking into remote wilderness areas, to the most modem version which consists of towing a "pop up" trailer to a stay for pay camp site and eating Big Macs and Church's fried chicken for a couple of days. Excess weight, shortness of breath, and a bad hip have all but eliminated the back packing trips for me, but I came up with a substitute that at least allows me to get back into the semi boondocks and somewhat removed from the ever present evidence of civilization found around every park area today. I call it "camping on the creek bank". In reality, it amounts to camping on the shoreline of creeks, rivers, lakes, etc. - anywhere that I can maneuver my 14' bass boat.

Before I leave on a camping trip I have carefully planned every need and have everything carefully packed so that when I arrive at the ramp I place all my camping gear, provisions, etc. into my boat before I back it into the water to launch. Generally if I am on unfamiliar water I spend a couple of hours cruising the shoreline searching for the perfect camp site. When I find something acceptable, I tie up at the bank, do some scouting, and if everything checks out I'll" unload,

SNAP TO MISTER!!

AS A RULE I TRY TO HAVE CAMP IN SHIP SHAPE BEFORE I START TO FISH.

I ALWAYS DIG A HOLE FOR THE FIRE PLACE.

I DON'T REMEMBER IT BEING THIS WAY WHEN WE WENT TO BED!

unpack, and get camp set up for comfort. As a rule, I try to have camp in ship shape before I start to fish.

One of the advantages of camping next to when you intend to fish is that you-can concentrate your fishing during the peak periods of bass activity and not send most of your time boat riding. If you have selected a nice, quiet and  ----- remote camp site, the hours spent around camp will be delightful and the naps you are able to take are beyond description. Anyone who hasn't stretched out on a hammock stretched between two trees in a quiet woods and taken a good nap just doesn't know what good snoozing is all about. I usually do my serious fishing at dawn and dusk and mostly loaf around camp during the day, unless, of course, the bass start making the noises previously described which always have the same effect on me. I instinctively jump in the boat and head for the "activity." During the hot weather, particularly July and August, I also fish for a couple of hours during the night. I usually camp out Friday and Saturday nights and am back home by church time on Sunday. I learned a long time ago that I ·could catch just as many fish by fishing only when they were active and biting as by spending all day on the lake, boat riding and thrashing the water. By relaxing and piddling around camp I am relaxed and rested

when I get home. Before I got older and wiser I would always return home sunburned, worn out, and with a splitting headache - not any more. I usually take a friend along, but occasionally go alone. Many who I invite are reluctant the first trip, but nearly all (except for a couple who I'll tell you about in a minute) are eager to go on succeeding trips, My camping gear consists of a two man tent, cots, sleeping bag, camp stools, lantern, ice chest, and a cook box that I built several years ago. It has legs that fold up for ease in travel and its door folds down to make a table top. If there is a chance of rain I also take a tarp along to stretch over the fireplace and cooking area. I also have a couple of canvas bags which I made to carry the groceries in. I always keep them tied up and hanging in a tree. Also I take a couple of collapsible plastic containers to keep drinking water in.

I always rely on mother nature for the fire. I dig out a hole for the fireplace and place the dirt and rocks around it. It is a good idea to gather your firewood supply while you are setting up camp and place it in a dry place out of the "traffic pattern". Gas stoves are nice but too much trouble to carry along for this type of camping. Most of us who have done much camping pride ourselves in our culinary talents. Some even guard their secret recipes - not me. Here are a couple that I'll share with you today:

BT's Scrambled Omelet (a breakfast special)

6 strips of bacon
1 potato
½ onion
Chunk of cheddar cheese
6 eggs
Picante sauce

Dice bacon, potato, and onion and brown in skillet - pour off grease. Add eggs and diced cheese and scramble till almost done - add salt. pepper and picante sauce and finish cooking. Devour and wash down with creek bank coffee. It'll hold you till dark if the fish bite all day.

BT's Famous Beans (good anytime)
4 strips of bacon
½ onion
Large can of pork and beans
Tomato sauce or catsup

Dice bacon and onion and brown in a skillet - pour off grease. Add beans and tomato sauce and some water. Let simmer long enough to get a fairly decent layer of wood ashes, grit, etc. on them before removing from the fire. Devour the beans and stay upwind of your partner the rest of the day.

There are many more good recipes but you can read them in my outdoor cook book which I'm working on.

One of my favorite creek bank camping spots is the cliffs along the west bank on the upper end of Possum Kingdom Lake. The reason I like that area so well is that it is remote and often the coyotes will serenade you at night as you sit around the campfire. Another favorite spot is a small knoll that extends out into the lake in the northwest corner of Millwood Lake. I like this spot because the bass fishing can be fantastic at times in that area, often you can catch them from the bank. There are good camping sites on the shoreline of Toledo Bend, Sam Rayburn, and most of the manmade lakes - particularly in the upper end of them.

It would be unfair if I failed to warn you of some of the unpleasant things which you occasionally encounter on these week end camp outs. These include mosquito's, spiders, and all manner of insects; snakes, frogs, turtles, coons, cats, stray dogs, etc.; torrential rains, oppressive heat, an occasional irate farmer or landlord, etc, etc. However if you persevere you will find ways to overcome each of these minor problems as they occur and it would take the fun out of it if I told you how to solve all the problems. Heck. you might as well stay at home and watch them fishing shows on T.V. Here are just a few of my wonderful experiences.

A former friend of mine went with me one weekend to a lake over in East Texas. Everything seemed to be going just perfect, It was early spring and he and I had worked hard all winter and had spent several weeks planning and talking about this trip. The appointed weekend finally arrived and the weather was just perfect as we left Dallas. We slipped away from the office at noon on Friday and drove over to the lake. We had carefully packed everything the day before so all we had to do was go by the house on the way out of town and change and hitch the trailer to the car. When we got to the lake we launched the boat and headed up the shoreline searching for a camp site. About a mile up the lake we found a good looking place. There was a clump of large trees on a hillside about a hundred yards from the water's edge. There as a natural boat dock where a log had washed ashore. There was a nice, level area where we could pitch the tent, a gentle breeze. and plenty of wood for the fire. Perfect.

Since we had been cooped up in an office all winter and this was the first outing of the spring we didn't spend much time getting the tent pitched and the rest of the stuff semi unpacked and sorted. We checked the lantern for fuel and decided we could finish up around camp after dark by lantern light. Wow! Did you hear that one splash? That was, ole Bucketmouth sure enough .... In ten seconds flat we were back in the boat and headed for the honey hole. Before long we were fishing, but not catching. Soon we decided to crank up and move further up the lake. We finally located an area that held a few fish and started catching them.

When the bass would quit biting we would tie on small Beetle Spins and Roadrunners and catch barn door crappie. The fishing was so good that it got dark before we realized it. We started back in the direction. of our camp ,but things sure looked different in the spotlight. We stopped several times to discuss how we were going to locate camp. Neither of us were familiar with the lake and we hadn't paid that much attention landmarks as we left. After wandering around for what seemed hours we finally located the log on the bank which was our "dock", When we got closer we could see the track left by the bow of the boat when we pulled it up on the bank. One thing that was peculiar was that we couldn't locate the tent with the boat's spotlight. We had a small flashlight with us so we started in the direction of camp. We got closer to where we both knew the tent should be but couldn't spot it with the flashlight either. My former friend was walking in front carrying the light and when we got to the campsite he yelled out "Oh sugar (or something like that), look at this mess!!! Our camp was in shambles - the tent was knocked down, all our gear was scattered and some broken, most of the food had been eaten. the ice chest was knocked over, and the entire area was dotted with horse apples. It turned out that we had camped in a "pony pasture." We gathered up what gear was salvageable and loaded it into the boat. While we were cleaning up the mess and loading the boat about a dozen Shetland ponies returned to the scene of their crime and watched us. The air got blue around there as we told them what we thought of their handiwork, (In hindsight I'm glad that was a fishing trip instead of a hunting trip). We finally made our way back to the launching ramp and put the boat back on the trailer and pulled it out of the water. We were hungry, tired. sleepy, and angry. But more sleepy than anything so

OFTEN THE COYOTES WILL SERENADE YOU AT NIGHT, AS YOU SIT AROUND THE CAMPFIRE.

we decided to sleep in the car and leave for home early the next morning, which we did. My former friend didn't say much the drive back and hasn't since.

There is another trip I remember very well because of a slight insect problem, My other ex-friend was along on this trip, I had let him select the camp site principally because he insisted, all 260 pounds worth, It was getting late when we arrived at the lake and we made a fast circle clear around the shoreline looking for a camp site. It was a small East Texas lake and sure looked fishy. We slowed down and were cruising the shore line on our second pass when he pointed to the spot of his liking. I headed the boat to shore not too pleased with his selection but in no mood to argue with the hulk. He had selected a level spot right on the bank next to an old dead tree. His idea was that firewood was right at the back door.

We unloaded right at dark and got the lantern going. Soon we had the tent pitched and I started unpacking things while he got a fire going. Before long things started to take shape and I cooked our supper. We ate a big meal and sat around the campfire and talked and drank coffee as we enjoyed the frogs - -croaking and other night sounds. The fire slowly burned down and there was no more firewood lying on the ground so the hulk got the hatchet out of a pack and walked over to the old dead tree and had chopped on it a time or two when I heard him scream like a panther as he raced back toward me and dove into the tent. Before I realized what had happened I was surrounded by irate yellow jackets which proceeded to sting me from head to toe. I ran to the lake and jumped in to get rid of my tormentors. The water was cold but by then it felt good - comparatively speaking. The yellow jackets soon found my ex friend in the tent and stung on him some more as he escaped to the shelter of the lake also. The water was not over our heads so we just stood in the lake and talked for awhile, trying to decide what to do next. Both of us were hurting pretty good and decided that we had better find a doctor. We climbed into the boat and headed to the car. We drove to three or four small towns before we located one with a small clinic where we received medical attention. We spent the night there and by morning were ready to go home. We hired a professional exterminator to go back to camp with us so that we could (he could) retrieve our tent and camping gear.

As previously mentioned, weather can also present problems. I took my neighbor's oldest boy with me one weekend. We had selected a camp site in a flat area in wooded hollow on the upper end of a lake in Central Texas. Everything was perfect. We had a neat camp (as the kid described it) and had stayed up late by the camp fire. He wanted TV learn all about earning from the expert so we talked and talked till I finally just went to bed and went to sleep. He shook me awake during the night and I at first thought he wanted to talk some more and was about to get irritated at him till I reached down to get my flashlight and felt water - lots of it. The kid was panicked; he had found a light and as he pointed it around the tent all you could see was water. Most of the gear had floated off and we

THE YELLOW JACKETS SOON FOUND MY FRIEND
IN THE TENT AND STUNG HIM SOME MORE.

would have too if we weren't on cots. The water was about a foot deep. The nice flat area we had camped was a dry creek bed and it had rained somewhere above us in the watershed that night and gravity did the rest.

We waded to high and dry ground and spent the night huddled around a fire that· I finally got started with my cigarette lighter. The sun finally got high enough in the sky to warm things up. I waded and swam to the boat which by now was out in the lake, With the boat I was able to retrieve most of the gear. I loaded the kid and we headed for the car. On the way home I made him promise not to tell his mom what had happened I don't think he did either for he went on several trips with me before he grew up and left home. In all my outdoor experiences I can truthfully say "There ain't nothing quite like camping on the creek bank - thank goodness".

CHAPTER 17

BRAZOS RIVER CATFISH – UP TO SIX INCHES

Back before World War II, my granddad and his family of six boys and three girls farmed outside Gause, Falls County, Texas. Grandmother had died right after giving birth to the youngest girl--Aunt Mildred.

Each spring during the rainy season while it was still too wet to plow, Granddad and the boys would hitch up the team to the wagon and haul an old flat-bottomed boat, which stood by the end of the barn all year, down to the Brazos River (or little River which ran into the Brazos) for a few days of fishing.

There were three good reasons for this annual expedition. First, Granddad loved to eat fish better than any human alive. Second, they could sell any "surplus" catch to the residents in Cameron for cash. Finally, It was a heck of a lot of fun.

Several days of preparation were necessary for a successful fishing trip. Granddad always planned each trip and assigned the responsibility of carrying out his plans as follows: Uncle Harley and Uncle Forrest would be responsible for filling the old boat with water and testing her for leaks several days in advance. Each leak was marked by a whittled peg, and the boat was turned over and the leaks mended with pitch or tar and punk.

They were also responsible for locating the cots (which had a habit of getting lost from year to year) and of hitching the team and loading the boat on the day of the departure. Uncle Stallard would be assigned to gathering up the fishing lines and tackle and getting it in good repair.

This consisted of getting a few old wadded and matted "trot" lines out, unwinding and unraveling them, and stretching them between trees. Needed hooks and sinkers were added and all of the old rusty hooks were sharpen-ed. An extra bale of stagin line was obtained for making bank lines up later or for making a few "pole" lines for anybody who might like to try their hand at bank fishing with a cane pole.

Uncle Roy would be assigned the job of gathering bait. This consisted of taking a spading fork down behind the hog pen and digging up some worms, getting Stallard to go to the little creek down behind the pasture to seine minnows and crawfish, and in killing two or three chickens so that they could have the livers, etc. for bait. (Incidentally, the girls would fry the chickens for them to pack for eats-but that was really the by-product.)

Uncle Tom would be responsible for getting the "camping gear" ready and packed. The gear consisted of a large tarpaulin which served as the tent, some old pots and pans which has been discarded over the years, a few gallon-size tin cans, and a kerosene lamp with a jug of kerosene.

Uncle Calvin would be responsible for helping the girls with the food to be packed. (Incidentally, these trips usually lasted only three days; but, if you would have observed all of the preparation, you would have thought they were going to be gone for a month or more.) The key to the food supply problem in those days was the mason jars. Nearly everything was packed in mason jars.

The box of food which was packed for the trip would usually consist of coffee, salt and sugar, bacon grease, canned vegetables--green beans, beets, corn, all packed in mason jars. Bread (biscuits and cornbread), meat--usually slab bacon and ham (plus the fried chicken), eggs and meal (to cook the fish) and many cakes and pies, which had been baked especially for trip. The cooking utensils consisted of an iron skillet, coffee pot, a gallon can or two, and two pans.

GETTING A FEW OLD WADDED AND MATTED "TROT" LINES OUT, UNWINDING AND UNRAVELING THEM!

On the appointed morning after the chores around the farm were complete (milking, feeding, etc.), there was a lot of hustle and bustle as each of the boys carried out his assigned task and, loaded the wagon and said goodbye to the girls. The farm was a few miles from the river, and it usually took three or four hours to drive the team and wagon to the camp site. Upon arrival, everyone again carried out his assignment in setting up camp and making preparation to fish.

The older boys would make the preparations to launch the boat and set out the trot lines and bank lines. The younger boys would get out a knife and go cut some poles and tie on the lines and start fishing. In a matter of minutes someone usually caught a . "perch" and started yelling, and the excitement would begin to mount. The "middle" boys had the unpleasant (at the time) task of tying up the wagon tarp so as to make a tent. However, it didn't take them long to have the camp in order and start fishing .

On one trip in particular, they caught a wagon load of fish (mostly catfish). They took tubs of the fish to Cameron to sell them. They were peddling  fish from house to house, and stopped at the Clark's house and knocked on the door. Uncle Tom was with Granddad at the time, and commented that the Clarks must have a foreign visitor since there was a Model A Ford parked their driveway with Michigan license plates. As it turned out, they did, for a foreign sounding gentlemen answered the door.

When granddad told him they were selling fish, he seemed interested. He said he was a relative of the Clarks, would be there a few days, and would like a good fish fry. He bragged a while about the great fishing where he came from. After they had discussed price and made a deal, the foreigner asked what size the fish were.

Granddad asked what size he wanted. He said, "How much do they weigh?" Granddad said, "We don't have a scale." He asked, "Well what size would you estimate?" Granddad replied, "Well, we got some up to about six inches."

"WHY... I MEASURE
THEM LIKE EVERYONE
ELSE IN TEXAS"!

With this-the foreigner broke up and really started laughing. He said, "Why, old man, I thought. you had fish to sell--not bait! In Michigan we use those sizes for bait."

Granddad said, "You sure must have some mighty big fish in Michigan." The foreigner laughed again at that comment and after a while began to sober up when he saw Granddad was quite serious.

He finally said, "Old man, It doesn't take a very big fish to eat a little six-inch fish. How did you- measure your fish anyway?"

Granddad said, "Like everyone else in Texas--between the eyes."

CHAPTER 18

THE "BLUE" HOLE – "NATURE'S CLASSROOM

My dad didn't become a fisherman until after he retired, and I started taking him fishing with me when I would go back home on vacation. However, I had some good teachers when I was a kid. My granddad was retired, and he would rather fish than eat when he was hungry. Most of the time, he took me and my two cousins with him on his fishing "expeditions." An expedition generally included at least two days of fishing and a night of camping out on the creek bank or lake shore.

One of Papa Bell's (my granddad) favorite fishing trips was to the "Blue Hole." The Blue Hole was near the highway overpass over the railroad-almost three miles from my uncle's farm. It was really the pit that resulted from digging the fill dirt to construct the highway overpass and was probably dug out around 1937 or 1938. It sloped from a shallow end down to a deep end, perhaps fifteen feet deep, and had a bluff running down one side of it. The other side was a woods. The water in the Blue Hole was unusually clear and had an aqua "tinge" to it - most said because there was a copper vein in the rock on the bottom of it. There were cattails, lily pads, and cane growing on the shallow end and scattered trees along the upper end. I would guess that the Blue Hole had about 40 to 50 surface acres. Because of the clearness of the water and the vantage point offered by the bluff, it was a near-perfect classroom to study the mysteries of what went on under the water. I shall never forget its lessons.

If you think ours is a tough environment, you should have seen the things I saw going on in the Blue Hole - snakes eating fish, turtles eating fish, birds eating fish, coons eating fish, fish eating snakes, fish eating bugs, fish eating birds, fish eating fish, etc., etc. (but not fish eating coons). I think they call this the "food chain," but to me, it appeared to be a case of the "big ones" always eating the "little ones" - no chain to it.

Some of the lessons I learned in general were:

1. Fishing generally wasn't much good on a clear, bright day-the fish were always in "hiding." (They were really just trying to stay out of the bright sun rays - just like we were by sitting under a shade tree.)

2. You hardly ever saw a catfish - they stayed in the deepest water and fed at night - except when a train passed! (When a train went by, the vibration started a chain reaction - crawfish, minnows, etc. started moving; bugs jumped in the water, etc., and the larger fish took advantage of the situation. Only a train or two per day traveled that rail line, however.)

3. The best fishing was generally on a cloudy, overcast day - when it rained, fishing was sometimes the best of all. (The rain apparently

dropped the water temperature slightly and added oxygen - thus stimulating activity.)

4. Bass, in particular, seemed to be just downright mean and ornery - the bullies of the "Blue Hole."   Most of the time that you got a bait or lure near them, they attacked!

Some of the things I observed about bass from the vantage point of the bluff were the following:

* On more than one occasion, I saw redwing blackbirds sitting on a cattail (singing to the bass, as Papa Bell would say) and see a bass jump out of the water trying to catch them.

* I have observed bass cruising around "wolf pack" style - trying to corner smaller bait fish. (It always seemed that the bass in such packs were of a uniform size - usually 2 or 3 pounders.)

* I have seen frogs leap into the blue water and a bass immediately give pursuit - and usually catch.

* I've seen small snakes swimming across the lake disappear in a big "slurp" as large bass came up out of the deep and almost nonchalantly open their mouths and suck them in.

* I've watched small bass rise to the surface to catch grasshoppers that made the mistake of landing on the water - yet, they made no attempt to catch snake doctors, nickel bugs, etc. (although the stupid little

bream would sometimes wear themselves out trying to catch these elusive bugs).

I've seen spawning bass attack everything that got near their "beds." They usually just "slapped" at things and didn't appear to be trying to eat them.

During the bass fishing craze of the '70s and now '80s, I have read many articles in magazines about most of these observations. I generally smile an inward smile and say to myself - "I knew that - I learned it at the Blue Hole many, many years ago."

MOTHER NATURE HOLDS SCHOOL IN THE BLUE HOLE!

F. UNCLASSIFIED

There are a couple of stories that didn't really fit in the other categories.

Old Wolf is a story told to me by my great granddad - William Thomas, it probably goes back 6 or more generations.

Trappin and Trainin Old Roosevelt is a true story based on my childhood experience.

And, the bear hunt is a collage of several hunting trips into old Mexico with a "punch line" from my all time favorite joke.

CHAPTER 19

- OLD WOLF -

.......I STARTED HAVING DOUBTS ABOUT OLD WOLF!

This story was told to me many years ago by my great-granddad, and it is probably one of the oldest tales that has lived through retelling by the Thomas clan.

One of our ancestors who settled in the wooded country around Linden in Cass County was Fate Thomas. They say that he was one of the best shots and the finest hunter and trapper in those parts. So the story goes -- he had a slight speech impediment--not bad, however, just s-s-stuttered a little bit.

One spring Fate caught an old she-wolf in one of his "snare" traps. When he found her, she was dead, of course; but there in some brush near the trap was a wolf pup. Fate noticed it only because, when he walked past, it growled at him--in a puppy sort of way. Fate started to hit it in the head and let it join its mother in wolf heaven, but the little rascal was so full of spunk and fight that he decided to keep him and try to raise him. After he skinned its mammy, he used the wolf pelt to throw over the pup and catch him. (Otherwise, he would have gotten wolf bit--the little feller had sharp tusks.) Af.ter he caught the critter in the pelt and started home with him, the pup finally quit fighting, growling, and yapping and went to sleep all cuddled up in the soft fur of his deceased mammy.

When Fate got to his log house, he yelled for his woman and young-uns to come outside and see what he had caught. With all the commotion the little wolf pup woke up, of course, and immediately bristled up and was ready to whup the whole crowd. Fate had to throw the pelt over him again to hold him and had his oldest boy to hold onto him while he went and got some wire and chain to tie him up with. After he had him securely. tied to the front post of the log house, he sent one of the girls inside to bring a bowl of fresh milk to feed him. The wolf pup probably hadn't nursed in a day and was powerful hungry. He lapped up the bowl of milk in nothing flat. Fate sent the girl back after more milk and a piece of venison meat. The pup consumed both of them; but when he finished, he was full and considerably more docile. Fate laid the peit down for him to lie on, and they all went inside the log house. When they peeped out directly, the little feller was sound asleep .

Fate told the family of his plan to "tame" the wolf pup and make a "huntin' dog" out of him. He warned the kids--particularly, the smaller ones--to stay away from him and leave him alone. Of course, that warning went in one ear and out the other; but as they got bitten, one by one, the lesson was soon learned; and, as the pup grew, it finally got to the point that the only one that could go near him without getting bit was old Fate himself. Fate continued to feed the wolf and to talk to him, and a sort of comradery developed between them. (It goes without saying that the wolf pup also learned early in life not to bite Fate; Fate had knocked him off his feet with his fists the few times that he had tried.)

When fall came, the pup had matured into almost a full-grown wolf-- even though he was still sort of "gangly" looking. Fate, for the lack of a better name, had started calling his pet "Wolf." A few times late that summer, Fate had taken Wolf walking through the woods with him. Whenever a squirrel or rabbit jumped up, he would take the chain off Wolf and "sic" him after it. If the squirrel ran up a tree, Fate would shoot it out, clean it on the spot, and let Wolf have the hide and inwards. If he shot a rabbit (which he rarely did), he would let Wolf eat him whole. (Rabbits in the summer weren't fit to ear-or, so folks thought in those days). He even let Wolf chase a few deer. With Fate's patience and

Wolf's instinct, the training was beginning to take hold and Wolf was. beginning to make a hunting dog. However, he never barked "treed" or nothing like that--Fate learned to watch his ears and hack to tell when "game" was near. Wolf had learned to depend on Fate for his "keep"; and even if he chased a deer for several miles, he would always return either to Fate, if he stayed In the woods, or back to the log house, where by now he had "dug himself a nice den up under the front porch."

When cold weather set in and Fate set out his traps and started running them regularly, he always took Wolf with him.

Near the dead of winter the Thomas household was running short on meat; and Fate decided he had better go kill a deer, bear, or something substantial. Bigger game had gotten scarce around the house; so he fixed up a knapsack of bread and stuff to take along in case they (he and Wolf) were gone for a day or two.

Most of the first day was spent walking--he had decided to head north toward the Red River country. They had seen very little game of any kind all that day, except for a fox squirrel which Wolf ran up a tree about sundown. Fate shot him for supper.

About dark Fate started looking for a good place to spend the night; and the first good holler he came to, they went down into it and found a good camping spot near a small stream and under some giant oak trees.

Fate cleared out a place and built a fire and cooked the squirrel. He ate all he wanted along with a piece of corn pone and washed it down with scalding hot tea which he had made. Darkness settled in, and the hoot owls started their nightly ruckus. Old Fate leaned back against the base of a big oak tree, lit up his corncob pipe, and watched the fire flicker. His stomach was full, the pipe was just right, and he was at peace. By and by, he heard a wolf howl away off in the distance--he noticed that old Wolf heard it, too, and was getting sort of restless; but he didn't pay it too much mind.

In awhile he got sleepy and decided to make his bed and go to sleep. He got up and raked up a pile of leaves for a bed. After he laid down, he remembered that he hadn't seen Wolf for a while; and he raised up on his elbow and called him. In a second he saw two eyes that looked like balls of fire out in the edge of the firelight, and Old Wolf came dutifully trotting over to him. He talked softly to Wolf for a minute or two, and Wolf finally laid down in the leaves beside him. Fate then drifted off to sleep land hadn't been asleep too long when he woke up--why, he didn't know immediately. He laid there wide awake in his bed of leaves, and the woods were as still in the crisp winter air and quiet as a cemetery. Off in the distance, but much closer than before, he heard a wolf let out a mournful howl. Almost Immediately, just a hundred yards or so away; he heard this wolf howl that made his hair crawl. It was his own Wolf, answering the pack, Fate wasn't the kind of man to get scared--but he was beginning to get concerned. He laid there listening and trying to decide what to do. He had his smooth bore Kentucky rifle beside him in the leaves--and that was a comfort to him. While, he was lying there trying to decide whether he should get up, build up the fire, and load his rifle or not, he heard footsteps off in the leaves and coming toward him. He reached down, slowly removed his knife from the scabbard, and laid real still and quiet to see what was coming.

As the thing came by the dying fire toward him, he could see that It was old Wolf; but by then he was getting might suspicious of that animal, so he decided to pretend he was asleep and see what would happen. As Wolf got closer to him, he slowed down to almost a stalk and came on up to the pile of leaves and circled around It a time or two. Then, Wolf came on up closer and started covering Fate up, head to foot, with leaves.

The wolf pack howled several times--much closer than before. Old Wolf trotted off a few yards, sat down on his haunches, and let out a long "Howwwlll" In reply. Then, he ran off through the woods In the direction of the pack.

By then Fate's mind was made up--he darn sure wasn't going to be a late supper for a pack of wolves; He got up, made a long pile of leaves where he had been lying, left his coonskin cap covered under the leaves so his "scent" would stay, built up the fire some, loaded his trusty rifle, climbed up into a tree, got into a good, comfortable shooting position in the first fork, and waited!

He could hear the wolfpack getting closer and closer and had barely gotten settled into the tree when he had them running toward the camp in the leaves. They stopped before they got to the fire, and he counted seven sets of eyes out by the edge of the firelight.

Directly, one of them started moving ·toward the pile of leaves. It was a terrifying sight to see that wolf, stalk slowly, slowly, toward where, but by the stroke of luck, he would be! He could tell without a doubt that the stalker\ was his huntin dog and pet--Wolf!

As Fate used to tell the story years ago--"W-W-Wolf j-ju-jumped on old F-Fa-Fate--and Fate wasn't thar--and I s-sh-shot him right twixt the eyes."

CHAPTER 20

TRAPPING & TRAININ OLE ROOSEVELT

If you think removing a half-grown, half hound dog from a steel trap which, is clamped tight on his front leg ain't one delicate task -try it some time. It's the best way I know of to get dog bit. That's exactly how I came to meet and own a half-redbone hound (other half unknown) that my dad named Roosevelt the day I brought him home .leading him with a piece of baling wire wrapped around his big neck. Even half-grown, he was one big dog and was double ugly looking. It took a lanky teenage East Texas farm boy to see the sub-surface beauty in him and to understand the possibilities of such an animal.

I spent the next few years trying to train ole Roosevelt, as I grew to manhood and he to doghood. The training process was one of my greatest challenges and in the end - I probably learned more than I taught. You see ole Roosevelt was, unbeknownst to me, doing a little training of his own - he was training me.

Times were sort of hard in San Jacinto country on a wore out farm about six miles cast of Pointblank in the late 30's and early 40's. The big war started in '41 and scarcity of many things - rifle shells in particular added to my many problems. One day I stopped at our neighbor's farm, sort of down in the mouth. Our neighbor and my idol, Uncle Josh White, asked me what was troubling me. I told him that I wanted a saddle for the old horse that my dad had let me start riding (bareback) but that I didn't have a dime nor any prospects of getting any money that I could think of. I told him that I had been to the Calhoun place, trying to get on at the sawmill but was told that I was too young.

I SPENT THE NEXT FEW YEARS TRYING TO TRAIN OLD ROOSEVELT!!

Uncle Josh was the-best hunter, fisher, and all round woodsman in that part of Texas at the time and he came up with a way for me to earn some money after he studied for a while ... trappin. We talked about trappin for a while and he figured out real quick that I didn't know much about trappin so he decided to take me on as a pupil and teach me. He said that all the signs indicated that it was going to be a colder than usual winter and that animal pelts should be good and thick. He figured that prices for pelts should go up also. His guess was that coon hides, might bring 50¢ a piece, fox pelts at least $2.00, muskrat about $1.00, and if I got lucky and caught a mink - upwards of $5.00. (He didn't mention possums, skunks, wild house cats, and stray dogs- all of which I became proficient at catching as it turned out). Anyway, while he was talking prices my mind was already catching mink, saving money, and had already picked out a new saddle and bridle with real silver trinkets on them.

Uncle Josh brought me back to reality with a command "meet me at my place at 5:00 am. in the morning and we'll get started." That meant that I would have to get up around 3:00 am. to milk and feed in order to meet his deadline. It was early December and Uncle Josh was right, it was cold the next morning, particularly at 3:00 am. It felt like a real "blue norther" had come to visit. I finished the chores at home and rode the old horse down to Uncle Josh's place. By the time I got there I was shivering, partly from the excitement of what lay ahead, but mostly from the cold air which had penetrated my own hide.

Uncle Josh was down at his barn. I saw the light from his lantern and went on down to the barn lot and turned my horse loose and went inside. He had a bunch of steel traps scattered on the floor and was testing them to see if they worked. They were old and rusted and he was placing the good ones in a burlap bag (toe sack) and cussing the ones that. didn't work, as he threw them in a heap.

Each time a broken trap clanked as it hit the pile, he would cuss again and spit tobacco juice half way across the barn. Finally he said "That ought to be plenty for an amateur like you - lets mosey on down to the creek". -I picked up the toe sack of traps and followed him across the barn lot and back pasture towards Stevens Creek. When we got to the woods we stopped and- he removed some birds (mostly sparrows) from a bird trap which he had set the day before. He popped their heads and put them in his coat pocket and we walked on.

When we got to the creek we turned north toward our farm and after we had covered about a mile we stopped and he made the first trap "set." He removed a piece of bailing wire from his coat pocket and wired the trap chain to a limber sapling. Next, he scraped away the leaves and scratched out a shallow hole in the faint game trail. He took a fresh chew of tobacco and then sprang and set the trap and placed it in the hole and covered it with leaves. Next, he took a bird from the other pocket and tied it to a limb over-hanging the-trap, The set complete, he explained that a fox would come down the game trail. smell the bird, and step in the trap while trying to get at the bird. That sounded good to me but as I'll tell you later, it didn't always work out like Uncle Josh explained it. We moved on up the creek a ways and he set another trap. This time, he talked while he worked and was explaining all sorts of things I should do - wear gloves which had been smoked over a wood fire to kill the scent, mark my traps so I could always find them, carry a gun when I ran the traps, always carry bailing wire in my pocket, etc. I either wasn't paying much attention or forgot his lesson for I later had to learn most of what he told me the hard way ... by experience.

We continued along the creek and set some traps in the water (for mink and muskrat) and some along the game trail - all the time Uncle Josh tried his best to teach me how to trap. After he had set .about eight traps he let me set a couple. The biggest problem I was having was springing the trap and setting the trigger. I very nearly lost a finger before I got the hang of it. He said "I've got some things to do at the house and must go, you can set the last two traps by yourself. You caught on real good." As he turned to leave he said, "Now you be sure to run this trap line every morning. come rain or shine, it ain't right to leave a critter caught in one of these traps all day long." I thought about what he said for several minutes - and decided that this trap line was going to be whole lot like a milk cow-confining!

I set the last two traps and studied for a minute - if my memory was correct, my trap line consisted of twelve traps strung along the east bank of Stevens Creek. The only mistake I made on the last two sets was, I forgot to mark them. I went on up the creek to our back pasture and cut across to the house. Mom was washing the breakfast dishes, She immediately lit into me for missing breakfast and not being ready for school. The bus was due any minute. My dad chimed in with "Where is the horse?" Saved by the school bus! It drove up then and I grabbed a cold biscuit and a piece of fried ham and lit out. I yelled and told dad that the horse was in Uncle Josh's barn lot as I boarded the bus.

The next morning I decided to run the trap line the first thing and milk and do the feeding when I got back to the house. I took the lantern and headed for Stevens Creek. However; since it was dark and I was running the trap line in the reverse order from the day before things didn't look the same. I must have spent an hour looking for the last two traps I had set the day before, and never found them. I finally gave up and went on down the creek and finally a marked trap set (there was a piece of. cloth tied in a bush near the trap). However, the trap was undisturbed and the bait was still tied over it. I sure was disappointed since I thought that each trap would catch something each night! How wrong that figuring turned out! My disappointment was short lived and I moved on down the creek to the next trap, and the next, and the next - each one undisturbed - until finally I saw success glowing in the light of the lantern. There were two little beady eyes shining from the place where I believed the next trap to be set. The adrenalin started pumping as I approached those eyes for I was confident that I had caught a $5.00 mink.

When I got close enough to see what I had caught, my spirits fell again, for it was a fat old possum. Since I had failed to bring a gun it was just as well. I sure wasn't afraid of a possum so I grabbed him by the tail, threw the sack over my shoulder and moved on.

It was already daylight by the time I found the last trap so I knew that I was running late again and in for more scolding from my parents. I started back to the house in a trot, lantern swinging in one hand and a sack with a possum in the other. By the time I arrived at the house, both mom and dad were madder than hornets.

It was already time for the school bus and again I had missed breakfast and had not cleaned up and got properly dressed - even worse, I had not milked or fed the stock. To add to my problems was the possum in the toe sack which needed to be skinned and stretched. While I was trying to decide what to do the school bus drove up. I threw the possum in the sack under the porch and ran for the bus with my mom chasing behind lighting the air to a brilliant blue with the terrible scolding she was yelling at me.

Things didn't go that well at school that day either, My mind was pre-occupied with that trap line. How in the world was I going to milk, feed, run the trap line, skin my catch, eat breakfast, and get ready for school all before that yellow bus arrived like clockwork each morning? Also, I wondered what reception awaited when I arrived home after school. I knew that it wouldn't be good.

When I stepped off the school bus I immediately smelled trouble. It smelled horrible. What could be the cause of that terrible odor? It seemed to be coming from the direction of the house - and was. As I neared the house I suddenly remembered the possum that I had tossed under the porch that morning. He was still there, tied up in the sack. However, he had a huge B.M. during the day and that was the source of the odor. I placed my school books on the porch and held my nose with one hand while groping under the porch for the toe sack with the other and finally got a hold on the sack. I gingerly pulled it from under the porch and started tippy toeing across the yard and toward the woods with it, hoping to escape before my parents saw me. When I got enough into the woods to be out of sight of the house, I stopped. It was decision time. It only took a second to decide - saddle or no saddle, I wasn't about to skin that stinking possum for a lousy ten cents! I was thankful that it wasn't a mink in the sack - that would have been a tough decision. I took my pocket knife and slit a hole in the sack and set the stinking possum free and went back to the house.

Fortunately, only mom was there and she was more concerned with the odor which she had been smelling all afternoon (but couldn't determine the source) than anything else and had forgotten the events of that morning. I told her I would try to locate the cause of the odor. After I changed clothes I went outside and broke off a couple of branches from a pine tree and snuck back into the house and placed them in the wood stove. I went back outside and got a couple more pine branches. lit them with a match, and held them where the wind would blow the smoke under the porch. Before long I had the house deodorized so well that you would have thought you were standing in a pine thicket. My mom was pleased with me, the odor was gone .

Dad had been gone all day and when he got home, that was another problem. He remembered the morning as well as the morning before. He called me outside for a stern lecture and the "laying down of the law." I either took care of my chores and was ready for the school bus each morning or there would be no more trappin - period! I kind a knew that was coming, for like I said, I had been mentally running through that morning routine all day while at school. I still had not come up with a solution.

I spent the next few weeks experimenting on different ways to accomplish all my early morning tasks and finally had it down to a science. I had added a step, a mid day nap at school instead of playing ball at lunch break. I even started catching a few varmints in the traps. The first two or three I caught were troublesome cause I didn't know exactly how to skin them or how to stretch the hides after I managed to undress the critters. As usual, Uncle Josh came to my rescue. He taught me how to skin each kind of varmint and showed me how to stretch the hides on pelt boards. He even loaned me several pelt boards of assorted sizes.

As previously noted, skunks, stray cats, hound dogs, etc. presented unique problems. After getting sprayed by a skunk, clawed by cats, and dog bit a time or two I finally learned how to deal with each problem as it arose. A carefully placed head shot to a skunk prevented any odorous aftermath when removing him from the trap. I learned that if you got the trapped cat or dog stretched out to the limit of the chain so they couldn't lunge at you it was a simple matter to walk up to them and throw a burlap bag over their head and grab them in a good enough hold to remove the trap before they got hold of you - usually. The owners of the hounds were another problem. By then, everyone in the country knew of my trap line and every time a coon or fox hound disappeared or came in skint up or lame you know who got blamed - me. However, my dad and uncles were all big men so no real harm ever came to me - just a few good cussings.

I had gotten so trappin wise that by Christmas I had figured how to take a vacation from the trap line. I sprung all my traps with sticks and didn't have to run the trap line till I reset them. Uncle Josh was real proud of I me when I explained that to him ~ although I thought I saw him wink to my dad as I was explaining. I also learned t at I could use meat scraps, chicken entrails, and other types of bait so I quit trying to trap birds for bait I had pretty much cleaned out the sparrow population around our place anyway and my mom had a hissy when she found out that I had trapped a few song birds for bait. I even spent 50¢ of my hard earned money for a bottle of mink scent which Mr. Orange had on special at the TEXO feed store where I sold my furs. That proved to be a good investment for I finally trapped a mink.

It must have been about the first week of February - I remember it was very cold that morning - that I came upon the trap with old Roosevelt in it. I remember that it was a Sunday morning so I was running he trap line a little later in the morning than usual and it was breaking daylight when I walked upon this large animal that was caught in my trap. When I first saw him from a distance it scared me for I thought I had caught a panther. There was always talk about panthers moving through our neck of the woods from time to time. I slipped a .22 hollow point shell in my trusty Stevens rifle and got up enough courage to move closer to the trap. Whatever was caught moved a little as I closed in and I very nearly touched off a shot. If rifle shells weren't so scarce I probably would have shot. Anyway, I didn't and was glad because I finally got close enough to see that it was a dog. A big dog! And he was one of the ugliest looking hound dogs that I had ever laid eyes on. True, he was large and very ugly; but the look in his eyes pleaded "help me" so I went on up to him. When I reached out to touch him however he almost bit my head off!! Instead, he bit my arm.

Again I contemplated using a bullet. Of all things, I had forgotten to bring a burlap bag with me that morning and didn't have anything to use to subdue the ungrateful critter with. While I stood there rubbing on my bit arm, that hound looked at me with his sad eyes and whined. That did it, I took off my coat and decided to use it. If he tore it to shreads, I had another ragged-old coat I could make it to spring with. I maneuvered him into position and threw my coat over his head and grabbed a hold of him. He started to fight and try to get loose - my, was he powerful - as I struggled to hold on and get the trap unsprung from his foot. We went round and round and I finally stepped on the trap spring by accident and released it. That big hound and me fell over backwards. I lay flat on my back with him a-straddle - finally, he reached down and gave me a big lick on the face and everything was fine except for his skinned and bleeding leg.

He didn't try to run off and since he didn't have a collar or any other evidence as to who was his owner I decided to take him home with me. Despite his ugly face and big head, I had already taken a liking to him and it appeared to be mutual. I figured he would follow me anyway but I decided to play it safe and lead him. I took a piece of bailing wire which I always carried and made a leash with it. After a little coaxing he started to limp along behind me as I finished running the rest of my traps. Since I was at the south end of the line I decided to stop in on Uncle Josh and see what he thought of my latest "catch".

As we approached Uncle Josh's house his hound dogs caught the scent of Ole Roosevelt and they really started a clamor. However, they were tied up, so noise is all they could create. Emmet, Uncle Josh's little spotted cur dog ran lose and he promptly came straight at Roosevelt and challenged him and lost. Emmet tucked his tail between his legs and lit out for the barn, yip yipping as he went. Uncle Josh by now had come outside to see what was causing all the commotion. When he saw me and the big ugly pup I was leading, he smiled his big warm Texas smile and came over to examine my new companion. He, too, took a liking to Roosevelt and pronounced that he would make a fine hunting dog and volunteered to help convince my parents to let me keep him. Uncle Josh, who was the local magistrate, pronounced him officially a "stray" animal by law and therefore mine to claim. And if anyone was an authority on stray dogs in the county it was Uncle Josh. He earned a part of his living by trading dogs, particularly coon hounds, and he probably knew every dog in the county. For sure, he knew every hound dog. He flatly stated that my new hound was going to make a fine cooner- somehow he could tell.

He went inside the house and returned with a pan of warm water, a jar of ointment, and some clean rags, While I held ole Roosevelt, Uncle Josh talked to him as only a hound dog man can as he dressed the wounded leg. Amazingly that dog never even acted like he thought of biting. It was as if he knew that Uncle Josh meant to help, not harm. When he had finished, I asked what he had said to the hound to gentle him down so? He said, "I told him that if he bit me I would bite back and reached in my pocket and showed him my teeth (false teeth of course)." I didn't know whether to believe him or not - he sure sounded convincing. Next, Uncle Josh went back inside and returned with a pan heaped with table scraps and cracklins. When he set the food in front of that starved hound I don't believe he was quite straightened back up before the pan was empty. Roosevelt really perked up now that his belly was full - his tail started to wag continually. From that day forward he learned that he could always stop at Uncle Josh's place for a "hand-out" anytime that he got real hungry. Uncle Josh had a real soft spot for hounds I general, and he really liked this new found double ugly hound in particular.

My spirits were high as I left Uncle Josh and headed home, leading Ole Roosevelt behind me. True, I didn't have that saddle or bridle that I had been working hard on my trap line to obtain - however, I had something better. I had me a real hunting dog of my own (providing I could convince my folks to let me keep him). As I got closer to home, doubts returned after all my dad already owned a pen full of hound dogs as well as several bird dogs. And of course a cur dog was standard equipment around any farm. The more I thought about it the more fearful I became that my dad wouldn't let me keep him. I had thought of all the things to say to win the argument. For example, "Untie Josh said he will make a fine cooner", and, "I can train him to fetch the cows", and, "I'll take care of him all by myself". As we walked into our front yard our reception was much the same as that received at the neighbors. My dad came out immediately and danged if he didn't smile when he got a look at Roosevelt. His first words to me were, "That looks like Roosevelt that you've drug up". I didn't know what he was referring to but his statement accomplished two things. First, it allowed me to keep the ugly hound and second it hung the handle of "Roosevelt" on him for the rest of his life.

It wasn't until about three years later that I found out why dad named my dog Roosevelt. I was along on a fox hunt and was sitting back away from the fire which the group of fox hunters had built to sit around while they enjoyed the hound dog music as well as a local product called moonshine. Anyway, I was nearly ready to doze off when I heard "Roosevelt" mentioned in their conversation which was interrupted occasionally by laughter. My ears perked up and I fine tuned in on their conversation and learned the reason I had got to keep my ugly looking hound.

My dad was one of a handful of admitted Republicans in that part of Texas and had been very vocal and outspoken in his criticism of the then president, Franklin D. Roosevelt. It didn't take much to set my dad off where politics was concerned, He couldn't understand how one man could be given the power to send troops over the country side to order the farmers to kill and burn livestock, plow up crops, agree not to plant, etc. In other words, dad didn't understand the "Ken." And it never helped him understand when the government started confiscating some of the land in the county and surrounding counties for natural forests and parks. Many of the farmers who sold out went to Houston and stayed, never to live on the farm again.

Most of dad's criticisms fell on deaf democratic ears. Matter of fact, he became the butt of some of their pranks and jokes and got into a few scrapes over politics. What I'm leading up to is that dad saw in my double ugly hound an opportunity to have something always around the place to cuss and call Roosevelt. And cuss and cuss he did However Roosevelt soon got used to it and didn't pay dad any mind when he would get on one of his political harangues and cuss Roosevelt for this and that. Matter of fact, dad became mighty attached to that hound himself. He would always insist on taking him on his coon hunts and when Roosevelt wasn't tagging along behind me he would be with dad if he was working outside, for he ran loose. He was special and not penned up with the other hounds and bird dogs, he was my pet and constant companion from the day I brought him home.

In general, he fit in pretty good with the other dogs on our farm except for the usual challenge from time to time. While he was growing up he got whipped a few times but as he neared maturity he was much larger and stronger than any of the other dogs so that any future confrontations became immediately "nolo contendre."

His first collar was custom made out of some discarded harness leather and I stayed up late several nights to braid a leash out of some rawhide. Roosevelt's leg was healed in a few days so I started leading him behind each morning as I made the round of running my traps; I could tell by his reactions whether a trap held a catch, long before we got to the trap. At first, he wouldn't get near a trap. I would tie him to a tree and go to the trap by myself. Finally he got to where he would go on up to a trap if it held an animal...but he never would go up to a plain trap.' My oh my, that hound was smart.

As a matter of fact. when I got back to the house with an animal I had trapped and started to skin it, Roosevelt would sit there on his haunches and watch intently as I went about the business of skinning the critter and stretching its hide on a pelt board.

That first year I took him along a few times when my dad and I went coon hunting. He wouldn't follow the hounds; instead he would casually saunter along behind. Dad would cuss his ornery, worthless hide;" He said that dog is too stupid and lazy to ever make a hunting dog - said he was the ugliest and sorriest excuse for a hound he had ever run across.

However, I knew that was not true and told him so in private (Roosevelt, I mean). I didn't have anyone to talk to most of the time so Roosevelt became my confidant. At times it appeared that he understood every word. He became a big help with the· chores around the farm. In no time I had trained him to go bring in the cows or horses. It didn't take long to train the cows and horses either. As I said, he was a large, powerful animal with an oversized head and strong jaws that could have bit a leg off a cow or horse if he was so inclined. His bark was worse than his bite, fortunately, cause I really would have had trouble explaining a three legged cow to dad.

Roosevelt shared one of my powerful dislikes - snakes. He became a good snake dog the next summer and killed several poisonous snakes - particularly along the creek when I would go fishing. One day a big cottonmouth moccasin bit him on the side of the head and I thought he was a goner for sure. His head, which was big naturally, swelled up to the size of a five gallon drum and he made it to the house and crawled under the porch and stayed. He went for several days without food or water and I went to Uncle Josh for help. I had tried everything I could think of to get him out. As always, Uncle Josh had a solution. He took a cane pole and attached the noose end of a rope to it and got down on his knees and worked the noose around Roosevelt's neck. It took both of us to pull him out from under the porch.   Uncle Josh immediately placed a big stick in his mouth and I helped hold him while Uncle Josh deftly lanced the side of his head with his pocket knife and let the head drain. He next poured about a quart of coal oil on the wound and forced some beef broth down him. He was soon eating and in a few days was as good as new and a lot wiser about snakes. He killed many of them thereafter and never got bit again, to my knowledge.

Roosevelt became the king of the hill so far as the other dogs in that part of the country were concerned. He whipped all of them that doubted. Every now and then a bitch dog would come in heat and for some reason she would invariably get loose from her pen, com crib, barn, or wherever the owner had placed her till the time passed. Most of those available females seemed to pass by our farm with their entourage following close behind full of hope. Now and then a fight would break out. Many were called but 'few were chosen, particularly if Roosevelt got wind of what was going on. When he joined the group it was nearly always as the chosen.

"OLD ROOSEVELT'S HEAD SWELLED UP TO THE SIZE OF A FIVE GALLON BUCKET"

DON KIRKLAND—85—

The next fall. there was a bumper crop of squirrels and I hunted them most every day. I always took he little cur dog with me cause he was an A number one squirrel dog. By then Roosevelt thought it was his right and duty to follow wherever I went so he started jumping the fence and following along behind .. just out of rock throw distance. He would watch the cur dog operate and in no time had figured out what I wanted. He got bold on the next hunt and walked beside me, watching the tree tops and listening for squirrels. When he located a squirrel he would slip quietly to the tree that held the squirrel and sit down under it and watch the squirrel. He would bark just loud enough to get my attention but not too loud so as to scare the squirrel. In the meantime, the cur dog was probably a mile away trying to find a squirrel the conventional way by smell and hard work. I soon learned that Roosevelt could locate all the squirrels I wanted and I didn't have to walk far to find him. I started leaving the cur dog home thereafter.

By early December, I had my trap line set and the first blue norther hit around the middle of the month. It was time to get serious about trappin again and try to make a few more dollars. I still didn't have that new saddle. Early that season the only thing I caught in my traps was coons. One morning when I was skinning a tough old boar coon the strangest thing happened. My knife slipped and I ruined the hide and I couldn't get it to stay on the pelt board. Ole Roosevelt was observing the procedure. I left the pelt board laying by the side of the smoke house, got ready, and went to school. That afternoon when I returned, he was waiting for the bus and as I got off, he tugged at my britches leg so I followed him. He led me directly to the smoke house where there was a big dead coon laying by the pelt board.

I petted him and bragged on him real good while I skinned the "replacement" coon that he had caught that day while I was at school. I made the mistake of bragging on his most recent accomplishment at the supper table that night. My dad really hoorayed me and got off on another of his long and colorful ridicules of that poor excuse of a democrat dog that I thought so highly of. I finished eating as quick as I could and excused myself from the' table. 1 sat and pondered the events of the day and wondered if Roosevelt really could think like a human.

The next morning I ran the trap line early and it was a dry run. I continued to ponder the prior day and had about convinced myself that my dad was not right about my democrat dog. But to make sure, I decided to try something when I got to the house. While I was thinking and walking I was also talking to Roosevelt as he walked alone beside me.

When I got to the smoke house, I went inside and picked out a mink pelt board and sat it beside the smokehouse and told Roosevelt that I wanted him to fetch a mink that day while I was at school. He looked up at me as if he understood. We would find out something today.

As before, when I stepped off the school bus that afternoon ole Roosevelt -was waiting. He sat there with a dog grin on his ugly face and his tail flopping back and. forth. He stood and started toward the smoke house with me close behind. He got there ahead of me so that when I walked up he was standing there with the purtiest mink in his mouth that you ever laid eyes on. I dropped to my knees and gave him the biggest hug I could. My heart was thumping - what a discovery I had made. I was so proud of him I could bust. I skinned the mink and stretched the hide but decided not to tell anyone of my discovery; not even Uncle Josh.

The next several weeks were the most productive pelt gathering period of my life.

Each morning, I would set a pelt board. or two by the side of the smoke house before I went to school; each afternoon when I returned there would be a critter that fit the particular board laying beside it coon, fox, mink, etc. It didn't seem to matter what type of pelt board J left out, he would "fill the order". Roosevelt was doing so well that I secretly took up my traps and quit getting up so early to run my trap line. During the day I would sit in class and try to guestimate how much money I already had accumulated in my unsold pelts and how much more I could make before the - winter was over at the rate we were going. My two fears where that someone would figure out what was going on and steal Roosevelt and that, at the rate he was going, he would catch all the fur bearing critters in. range before winter was over. I also got to daydreaming a lot about what all I could now afford - new rifle, Stetson boots, and of course, the saddle and bridle - maybe even a cutting horse.

But as I learned again and again later in life, when things get to going too good, look out! Disaster is just around the next corner. One day as I was coming home from school on the bus I got this funny and uneasy feeling. When I jumped off the bus Ole Roosevelt wasn't there to meet me and I almost cried. I immediately started calling him but he didn't come. I ran into the house and asked mom and dad if they knew where

Roosevelt was. Neither remembered seeing him since morning and dad commented that he did seem to be acting sort of peculiar when he saw him down by the smoke house.

I dashed outside and ran to the smoke house. When I got to the smoke house the thing I saw sent a chill up my spine. There sitting next to the mink sized pelt board I had sat out that morning was mom's old ironing board. One of the legs on it was busted and my dad had left it setting beside the smoke house while he made a new leg to repair it I now knew what had happened to my great hound dog. He had examined that ironing board carefully, before he headed off to the woods to catch a critter that would fit it. No telling where he was. I never saw or heard from Ole Roosevelt again and I don't know for sure what happened to him. He might have strayed south into Mexico or north into Canada before he found something that would fit that ironing board. As big and strong as he was, I doubt that he could have killed a grizzly bear or mountain lion by himself. Or he might just have spent the rest of his life wandering around the woods. in -East Texas, looking for a non-existent giant coon or something. I just don't know.

I'm inclined to believe it was the latter because I go down to the Sam Rayburn lake country occasionally and every time I do I see more ugly looking hound dogs than elsewhere in the state. I'm sure that Ole Roosevelt's genes are in all of them. I've thought a time or two about stopping and picking one of the ugly critters up, particularly when I see a young stray. But then I pause and conclude, Ole Roosevelt was enough hound dawg for a lifetime, particularly for a Republican.

CHAPTER 21

BEAR HUNT IN OLD MEXICO

Paddlefoot Thomas was an avid hunter. He probably enjoyed hunting more than anyone In our part of the country--Sunset, Montague County, Texas. He spent his life on a one horse farm just north of town and hunted at every opportunity. However, around there, hunting was limited mostly to small game and varmit--rabbits, squirrels, quail, coons, and coyotes.

Whenever the men folk gathered at the domino parlor, talk soon drifted to hunting and fishing tales.

Paddlefoot could tell tales that were exciting and authentic. He always ended by saying, "Boys, I've hunted round here all my life and enjoyed every minute of It--but before I die I sure want to go big game huntin' at least once."

When he said that, a far-away look would come to his eyes and everyone would get real quiet for a while. They all knew how bad Paddlefoot wanted to go big game huntin but all figured It was an impossible dream. There wasn't- any "big game'" for many miles from Montague County and nobody, particularly Paddlefoot, had the means to travel very far back In the '30's.

By a stroke of luck (or fate), Paddlefoot realized his impossible dream. One of the Croft boys who had been coon hunting with Paddlefoot many times got an important job with the railroad. He traveled mostly, but came back to Sunset the next Christmas and delivered an envelope marked "Merry Christmas" to Paddlefoot.

Paddlefoot thanked him, opened the envelope, and asked, "What the dickens is this?" (He couldn't read or write). The Croft boy said, "It's your big game hunt." Paddlefoot looked puzzled, so Croft went ahead and explained that It was a railroad pass and it would allow him to ride the train to a place where he could go big game hunting.

The Croft boy also said that he had gotten acquainted with a boy from Del Rio, Texas, whose sister was married to a rancher In Coahuila, Mexico, where they had both bears and mountain lions. The rancher had Invited Paddlefoot down to help rid his ranch of the critters that killed his livestock. The Croft boy told ,Paddlefoot to be ready to travel the day after Christmas and that he would ride the train to Del Rio with him.

Soon enough, early the morning of Dec. 26 the Croft boy and his Pa picked Paddlefoot up In their wagon and headed for the depot at Bowie.

Everybody turned out to see them off at the Bowie depot. The local weekly newspaper editor was there and took pictures for the article which he wrote for the week's issue of The Bowie Progress.

Everything went as planned, and Paddlefoot was off on his dream. He was gone for two weeks. When he returned, it was late at night; and -- none met him at the depot. (Like I said, he couldn't write and probably didn't realize that telephones could talk past Bowie.) Anyway, he walked about twelve miles) and got his horse and wagon and went back to the depot to pick up his guns and belongings. He had lots of chores to catch up on; so nobody saw him in several days.

On- the second Saturday, however, he showed up at Purcell's General Store In Sunset. Immediately, he was besieged by everyone there to tell about the big game hunt. He promised to tell the story after he got some chewin tobacco and a Nehl soda water. The word spread like wildlife, and, In no time Purcell's General Store was packed for the memorable event.

Paddlefoot began to get some-what bashful at the crowd and was about to back out of telling his story.

However, Cecil Brown started proddin' him with, "What kind of luck did you have? Old you miss any shots?" Finally, Paddlefoot said, "Wal-- there wasn't much to It, not enough to tell that I can remember." Cecil said, "Well why don't you just start from the time you left Sunset and just go from there?"

Paddlefoot finally said, "Wal--OK. Here's what happened. Me and the Croft boy got on the train at-Bowie and she tooted a time or two and lit out. We'd ride for a while and stop for a while, and It seemed like this went on forever. I looked out the winder several times afore dark; and, generally, about all you saw was pasture fields with a few cows or hills; and a time or two when we stopped, It was at little old towns about like Bowie. Finally, I got tired and shut my eyes for a nap and listened to that cllckety-clack of the rails and went sound to sleep.

I didn't wake up till the Croft boy was stabbin' me and said, "We're here--we're In Del Rio." I looked out the winder and It was dark outside; but I could see lots of folks under the lights milling around and some fellers pulling little wagons around with sacks and boxes on them. I gathered up my belongings,· and we got off the train. We went Into a little eatin place there at the train station and had some coffee and bacon and eggs, and I was feelin right pert after that.

However, the. Croft boy said I was on my own--that he had to go to work at 6 a.m. (It was about 5:30 a.m. then). He told me to sit tight at the depot and that one of the ranch hands would pick me up around 8:30 a.m. and take me across the border to the Mencer Ranch.

It was gettin light so I wandered around the depot and tried to strike up a conversation but my Spanish was too limited to get far. I wanted to ask about the bear hunting In Old Mexico but couldn't· think of the word for bear. (Oso--I found out later.)

After what seemed like six hours an old busted up Model A drove up and a lanky looking feller got out and walked straight to me. I don't know how he picked me out. Anyway, after "Howdys" he asked If I as the feller going bear huntin' and I allowed as how I was. We loaded up my belongings In the Model A and he hid my 30-30 under the seat. He cranked her up and we headed south. In a few minutes we came to this bridge and had to stop on both banks.

The cowboy talked in English on this side and Spanish on the other side. Whatever he said seemed to please everyone for soon the bridge was at our backs and we were headed south Into ranch country. We stopped at about ever windmill and water hole to water the Model A--It had a radiator leak. By late afternoon we started driving some rough roads up into the mountains. The country-side was purty as a pup and I knew I was going to enjoy my visit and bear hunt. But some of the narrow ledges on the sides of the mountain were real scary. If you went off the road you would have dropped almost a thousand feet - straight down.

He rounded a bend In the road and up ahead In a box canyon was an adobe house with wood smoke coming out the chimney and the aroma of meat frying mixed with the wood smoke smell reminded me how hungry I was. All we had eaten that day was some Jerky. When we pulled up In front of the house and stopped this big burly man, buxomy woman, and little boy came out to greet us. The man put out a ham sized hand and said, "Name's Zeke Menser, this Is the misses, and that's our son Tony. Welcome to Menser ranch:" I introduced myself and we went inside and washed up. We set down to a supper fit for a king.

After we ate, we went outside on the porch and lit up our pipes and started talking (hunting talk mostly). I finally got around to braggin a little about what a good shot I was--that I usually shot squirrels through the eye with my .22 or else "barked" them so as not to mess up any of the meat. Zeke allowed as how he didn't waste his time with squirrels, since the mountain was full of bears, Javelna, mountain lions, and deer. He said they would see what kind of shot I was trying to shoot at a big old bear's eye out -especially if he was charging down the mountain at me to bite my head off. I gulped and swallered a cud of tobacco at the thought.

Tony said, "Paw can I take Mr. Thomas out early In the morning to shoot some quail and rabbits to eat." He has a .22 with him. Zeke said, "No boy, he came down here to go bear hunting". J could tell that the boy wanted to find out what kind of a shot I was so I said, "I'd like to go out early In the morning with the boy to kind of get the lay of the land--I've got a week to bear hunt." Zeke said OK so we all went to bed.

Next morning after breakfast, I got out my .22 rifle and some cartridges and Tony and I lit out. We promised to return by mid morning with a mess of quail and some rabbits.

We started on around the mountain toward a thicket and I took the lead 'cause the trail was getting a little growed up with brushes and briars and it was gettin to be a man sized job pushing the limbs and stuff out of the way to get through. It was sort of spooky in that tangle for we smelled what I thought was hogs; but the boy said it was bear smell and you couldn't see too fur in any direction. I had just parted some brushes to step through when this giant of a bear reared up right in front of us--I mean me 'cause that Tony lit out back down the path like a scared rabbit.

Me and that bear stood there about eyeball to eyeball for what seemed like ten minutes, and he finally let out a deep GRRROWWLL! I messed in my pants. " The crowd had been spellbound at Paddlefoot's tale up to this point. The silence was finally bronken by Slim Nelson, who said, "Wal, Paddlefoot, that ain't too unusual or reason to be ashamed. I mean, most any man here would probably have messed in his pants too If he met a big mean bear up on the side of a mountain that close up with just a little .22 rifle for protection."

Paddlefoot said, "Shucks, Slim, I don't mean then--I mean just now when I went GRROWWLL!"

The end.

That's all folks - time to buy another of Bill T's books.

- 207 -

BOOKS WRITTEN BY
BILL R. THOMAS

Title	Brief Description
1) A Summer on Piney Creek	A Summer Spent with Friend Living in a Cave on Piney Creek (Kentucky)
2) Hickory Fired Tobacco, Moonshine Whiskey, Beautiful Horses, and Fast Women	Kentucky Based Short Stories
3) Bill T's Texas Bob Tales	Texas Based Short Stories
4) I Smell Smoke	Authors Experience as B-47 Crew Member in Strategic Air Command
5) My Most Memorable Adventures - One Hunting and One Fishing	Hunting Trip in Mexico and Fishing Trip in Alaska
6) The Accumulated Wisdom of the Bugscuffle Domino, Whittle and Spit Club	Philosophy and Wisdom Gained Over a Colorful Lifetime
7) The T-Bone Ranch	Developing a Cattle Ranch in Montague County, Texas
8) A Wild Shot In The Dark	Autobiography - Birth Through Air Force
9) The Debits Are On The Left, The Credits Are By The Window	Autobiography - Air Force to Present

www.ingramcontent.com/pod-product-compliance
Lightning Source LLC
Chambersburg PA
CBHW022018090426
42739CB00006BA/190